Dividend Investing for Beginners

Build your Dividend Strategy,
Buy Dividend Stocks Easily, and
Achieve Lifelong Passive Income

G.R. Tiberius

TO MY WIFE AND MY SON, THIS BOOK IS FOR YOU

Table of Contents

Introduction

"The less money lying idle, the greater is the dividend." — *Walter Bagehot*

Stock markets have always attracted people who have been searching for financial freedom. This makes sense since the market has been one of the greatest creators of wealth the world has ever seen. Over the past century, American markets have risen by 10% annually (Sullivan, 2020). A sum of $1,000 invested 100 years back would have grown to $13,780,612 by now.

While investing 100 years ago was optimal, you have to make do with market conditions in the present, since it's not as if you could go back in time and invest your money. Herein lies the rub: how can you be rest assured that the markets will continue to rise? Is there some way of guaranteeing a return over a long period of time, no matter what happens in the broader market?

Before providing the answer, I'd like to point out that there are no guarantees in the markets. I can appreciate how bad that sounds. After all, when I began my investing career, I had the same question. However, the sooner you realize that risks exist in every investing venture, the easier you'll find it to make money.

This is because extreme risk aversion only results in you chasing unrealistic investment schemes. There's no shortage of these schemes out there, and all of them promise to make you 10% or more every month with little downside. The truth is that all of these schemes are castles in the sky. They're not realistic, and chasing them will only lose you money. Instead, you need to accept the reality that if you're investing in the stock market, you'll have to absorb some risk.

This isn't to say you should build an extremely risky portfolio. Instead, your task is to build a portfolio that contains some risk, but not too much. The definition of "too much" risk varies from one person to another, which is why no two investors' portfolios look the same.

Risk-averse investors might be satisfied holding onto two positions, while more aggressive investors might hold 10 positions; it all depends on your risk appetite. However, no matter what your appetite is, there's no doubt that investing in dividend paying stocks and instruments is one of the best ways to grow your wealth over the long term.

Why Dividends?

Imagine you own something, and every now and then, it pays you cash. In addition to paying you cash, it also grows in value over time, thereby giving you two ways of making money with it. If you've dabbled in real estate investing previously, you'll recognize this sort of an asset. It's how a piece of property behaves, after all.

In the stock market, you can invest in dividend paying instruments to replicate this performance. Dividend investing is thrown about a lot in investment education circles as a silver bullet. I must mention that this strategy isn't a guarantee of riches in any way. There is risk involved.

However, compared to other forms of investing, dividend investing minimizes risks and leaves investors with a good probability of making money. It certainly isn't some get-rich-quick scheme. However, it's not a risky investment strategy either. In this book, you'll learn why this is the case, and how you can structure your portfolio to incorporate these characteristics in it.

There are no barriers to investing in dividends. Whether you have just $100 in your account or $10,000, dividend investing scales to any dollar amount of capital. Many investment strategies that promise high returns stop working when the capital invested in it becomes too large. After all, the greater the capital, the tougher it is to produce above average market returns.

Dividend investing is great because it works no matter how much capital you have. Best of all, you can set your portfolio on autopilot and forget about it. Your portfolio will keep jogging along in the background making you money, while you focus all your energies on whatever interests you. Thus, if you're looking to build passive income streams, dividend investing offers a great way forward.

Note that it takes a while to build enough passive income from dividends to pay for your lifestyle, even up to a year or more. Think of it as a marathon, rather than a short sprint. However, if you stick to it and follow the principles in this book, you'll end up creating a stream of wealth that will sustain you for a long time.

Many investors sabotage themselves because of a lack of patience. They want gains and riches right now and end up investing most of their money chasing hot stocks and other charades, such as penny stocks or cryptocurrencies. The only thing guaranteed in these ventures is that they involve a lot of luck, most especially if you don't understand them. Skill matters a lot in understanding these types of instruments, but more importantly, you should only put the money that you can afford to lose into them.

Dividend investing is boring, exactly how investing should be. It's not going to give you sleepless nights, and it's not going to be like strapping yourself to a rollercoaster. You're not going to check in on your portfolio more than once a month. In fact, you can automate investing to such an extent that you don't need to check in more than once a year.

If this sounds good to you, then dividend investing is the perfect strategy for you. Let me put it this way: If someone told you there was a way to make a million dollars by putting in some work in the beginning and then sitting back and doing nothing else, would you take it? That's what dividend investing is.

My Journey

My investing journey began five years ago, and since then, I've been passionate about teaching people all about the wonders of dividend investing. My goal is to build a retirement nest egg that's going to last me a lifetime and will help me achieve financial independence. Retirement is on my mind, and passive income is the vehicle I'm using to create a life that I want.

Don't get me wrong, before I achieved what I have now, I lost literally millions. I was a victim of all these get-rich-quick schemes driven by my curiosity and emotion, and unfortunately, by trusting the wrong people. It was a terrible yet life-defining phase in my life. From there, I took all the lessons I could absorb to come back, recover, and thrive.

I believe that dividend investing has the power to transform people's lives, if they just give it a chance. I've seen so many people derail themselves chasing get-rich-quick schemes, and it frustrates me no end. You don't need a special education or high IQ to succeed as a dividend investor. Key to note that I am not a financial advisor, my purpose here is purely educational and to share the lessons that I have learned along the way. It is best to do your own research and if needed, consult with a professional for specific plans on your investments.

Can you add? Multiply? Divide? Subtract? If you answered yes to those questions, congratulations, you're fully qualified to be a dividend investor. Many people overcomplicate the investing process, which is why I've written this book. My intent is to show you that you don't have to overthink investing.

Instead, all it takes to make a lot of money is following a few basic principles and you'll be just fine. So, without further ado, let's dive in and explore what exactly these mythical dividends are.

Chapter 1:
Dividends and Dividend Stocks

So, what is a dividend, and why is it so special? To answer this question, we need to step back and examine what a stock is. Stock is a collection of individual shares, and a share is literally a piece of a company floating around on a public market. Companies sell shares of themselves to raise money from investors, then use that cash to fund their businesses.

Owners of shares receive benefits, but also run some risks. For starters, they receive the right to partake in the profits that a company generates. However, they're also exposed to any losses that the company incurs in due course of business. This is in contrast to a company's creditors, who are paid interest no matter what happens.

Thus, stock ownership is a high-risk, high-reward deal. Note that the term high risk here is relative. The risk of owning stock is greater than owning a company's debt, or bonds. Some companies are riskier to invest in than others. For instance, a new company that has never made money in business is riskier to invest in than a company like Coca-Cola, which has been around for ages.

Coca-Cola is a stable company that has a well-established brand and business model. While it might suffer from downturns every now and then, the odds are on its side. In investing, you must focus on the odds of success, as opposed to the certainty. There are no certainties in the market, which is why great investors focus on lining up the odds on their side before investing their money.

Returning to stocks, some companies are more stable than others, and generate a ton of cash via profits. A percentage of these profits are reinvested back into the business to produce even more profits. For instance, if you're running a lemonade stand, you'll reinvest those profits to buy more lemons, sugar, water, a new stand, and so on.

Let's say you have some cash leftover once you've bought all of these things. You can leave some cash lying around in the bank to account for emergencies. What if you still had some cash leftover? You don't have any use for it, so it makes sense to pay yourself a special "dividend".

This is where dividends come from in larger companies as well.

What are Dividends?

In accounting terms, a dividend is a payment that a company makes to its shareholders. This payment can be cash, stock, or even property. However, cash dividends are the most common, and property dividends are almost nonexistent. In an ideal world, a dividend payment is made after the company has accounted for all of its reinvestment needs.

The logic behind a dividend payment is that if a company has no use for cash, its investors must be given the opportunity to make use of it through another venture. Let's say you've invested a sum of money with a company and it has $1,000 leftover. If the company doesn't need it, they can pay you that sum, and you can invest it in something else where it will grow. In essence, that's why companies pay dividends.

Dividends are paid in proportion to your stock ownership. Therefore, someone who owns more stock than you will get paid more. I'd like to point out that companies are not obliged to pay dividends; for instance, a company that is growing fast is unlikely to pay dividends. Growing companies need all the cash they can get their hands on, and are therefore best served hanging onto it.

Some companies don't have a need to hold onto cash, but refuse to pay dividends anyway. You'll soon learn why this happens. For now, understand that the decision to pay a dividend lies entirely with a company's management. Investors will have to call a shareholder vote and win a majority to push company management to release a dividend payment.

A good example of this occurred in 2012, when Apple finally decided to pay dividends to its investors. The company had more cash than it could make use of, but thanks to holding this cash in offshore accounts in Ireland, it couldn't release it to investors without incurring huge taxes. Apple was initially content to simply sit on this cash pile and do nothing.

However, investors led by hedge fund activist David Einhorn summoned a vote and pushed Apple to pay a dividend from that cash pile. Apple eventually borrowed money from American institutions, offset that debt against its huge cash pile, and paid investors a dividend.

Some investors like to paint dividends as being good all the time, but the truth is that every circumstance is different. In Apple's case, paying a dividend was good. However, there have been instances where a dividend payment has been bad for shareholders. To understand why this happens, it's worthwhile to take a look at how the stock market values dividends.

What are Dividend Stocks?

Dividend stocks are stocks that pay out dividends. A company that pays a dividend is often stable and has enough of a cash hoard to sustain its business. This can be a curse and a blessing for its management. Once a dividend is declared, the market tends to value the stock highly, and its prices fluctuate less since it comes to be viewed as a stable company. If the broader market suffers from a downturn, dividend stocks tend to hold their prices much better than those that don't pay dividends.

Thus, a dividend can boost a company's perception and valuation in the market. However, investors come to rely on the steady dividend payments as a sign of stability. If the dividend decreases or is suspended, there's usually hell to pay in the markets because it triggers a wave of selling in the stock.

This usually happens due to the way institutional finance works. Large investment funds allocate their assets within strict parameters. For example, some funds must allocate 10% of their overall capital to a dividend paying stock within a sector. The criteria for this investment must be a company that has maintained its payment for a certain number or years, and it must fulfill size requirements or other guidelines.

If a company suspends its dividend or doesn't maintain it at the same levels as in the past, it runs afoul of these criteria, and the institution has to sell its shares. Given that they own a few hundred millions to a billion, it triggers a huge wave of selling and the stock price falls. This fall, in turn, pushes smaller investors to sell out of a sense of panic.

The news announcement of a dividend suspension also triggers its own wave of selling. Overall, once a dividend is declared for the first time in a company's history, its management makes it a priority to maintain it no matter what. In many ways, a steady dividend payment overtakes business needs.

A good example of this almost occurred with Boeing in 2020. Boeing had been having a rough few years since 2015, thanks to the disastrous rollout of its 737 Max airplane. Fatal crashes, complaints of unsafe quality controls, and management ignorance pushed its stock price downwards. Throughout all of this, despite smaller profits, Boeing's management maintained its dividend when the better move might have been to hold onto cash, reduce or suspend the dividend, and reinvest that money into the business.

Think of it this way: If you're running a lemonade stand and are facing tough business conditions where you know you'll need more cash to maintain your business, would you voluntarily pay yourself a dividend bonus? Most business owners wouldn't, but Boeing's management did this because they were concerned about the stock price tanking if they reduced the dividend.

However, worse was yet to come. 2020 arrived and the pandemic wrecked the airline industry, Boeing's biggest customers. With orders falling to zero, Boeing posted a huge loss and the question of the dividend once again rose. Some investors, primarily uninformed ones, thought that Boeing ought to borrow money and pay investors a dividend to maintain the stock price.

There are logical gymnastics, and then there's that point of view. The idea that a business ought to go into greater debt when it was struggling to make money just so it could prop up its stock price shows how dividend payment histories can warp minds. Thankfully, Boeing's management did the logical thing and suspended the dividend. The stock price fell, but it wasn't as if the fall was not justified, given the state of the business.

When evaluating dividend-paying companies, you'll often run into such scenarios where management maintains the dividend for the sake of it, and not for the sake of the business' health. This isn't necessarily a sign of poor management, as it reflects the irrational ways in which the market looks at dividends sometimes.

Having said that, there are some clear advantages to investing in dividend-paying companies.

Dates

A company that pays a dividend follows a well-documented process that investors can track. This process is governed by a series of dates. The first date to note is the declaration date, which is the date when the Board of Directors declare their intention to pay a dividend. This announcement typically mentions another date called the ex-dividend date.

The ex-dividend date is the most important one of them all. This is the first day that the stock trades without the right to receive a dividend, and usually occurs two days before the record date. On this day, the price of the stock will be reduced by the amount of the dividend. If you purchase a stock on the ex-dividend date, you won't receive a dividend until it is declared for the next time period. To be able to get the dividend, you have to buy the stock before the ex-dividend date; if you purchase a stock even one day before and sell it on the specified date, you will be entitled to receive the dividends.

Two days after the ex-dividend date is the record date. Many new investors confuse the record date for the ex-date. The record date's definition has something to do with this. The record date is when the Board compiles a list of shareholders to determine who receives a dividend. Beginners confuse this compilation process for the determination process. Instead, the best way to think about the record date is to think of it as a list-building day.

During this day, the company looks over their records and figures out who held its stock before the ex-date. Next comes the record date, on which they compile those names into a list. Finally, we have the payment date, which is self-explanatory. This is when investors as of the ex-date receive payments.

These dates have a significant effect on prices. Usually, the price of the stock decreases by the declared dividend amount before the ex-date. It rises back up after the ex-date since buyers at this point won't earn the dividend. You might think there's a profitable strategy here where you buy a stock before the ex-date, capture the dividend, and then capture the rise back up after the ex-date.

The problem, however, is that everyone else in the market is aware of this, and you're not likely to make much money due to prices being inflated. Besides, these short-term tactics don't make money in the long run. It's best to stick to the basics and remain invested for a long time, and to avoid trying to outsmart yourself.

Why Invest in Dividend Stocks?

Dividends have played a significant role in the returns investors have received during the past 50 years. Companies that have paid dividends have experienced the highest growth since 1973.

Dividend Stock vs Growth Stock vs Dividend Growth Stock

Any stock that pays a dividend is a dividend stock. They're stable, mature, and believe that future growth is limited, so it makes more sense to pay dividends to shareholders. They're safe companies and are great choices for risk-averse investors, since they're less volatile and offer safe cash flow. IBM and Coca-Cola etc are good examples of this.

Dividend growth stocks are a type of dividend stock. They issue dividends at lower yields and are cheaper than regular dividend stocks. However, their annual payouts increase, making them attractive long-term investments.

Growth stocks are companies that are still experiencing high growth and don't pay dividends, meaning that they have plenty of opportunities for expansion. Examples of such companies include Amazon, Nautilus, and Alibaba.

Advantages of Dividend Stocks

An investment that pays you via price increases (capital gains) as well as cash flow (dividends) is bound to have a lot of advantages built into it. Here are some of them in no particular order.

Stability

Investors who are looking to minimize risk in their portfolio often turn to dividend-paying instruments, since they tend to be more stable in the long term. A company that pays a dividend is typically well established in its industry, so it usually doesn't have too much competition. Even if it does, it probably has them well under control.

As a result, during bear markets (a term used for when markets fall), dividend stocks don't decline as much. In some cases, their prices even rise a little because they're viewed as safe havens. For instance, look at a company like Coca-Cola. It has a product that will not go out of fashion whether times are good or bad, a giant marketing machine working in its favor, and has just one large competitor in Pepsico.

It has a brand name that is recognized everywhere in the world, and has a slew of subsidiary businesses that have equally strong brand names. As a result, it has a strong portfolio that will help it tide over any tough times. During good times, it probably won't keep pace with the hottest stocks in the market, but it's not as if it's going to fall precipitously.

Stability also extends itself to management. The managers of such companies are typically people who have worked in them throughout their careers. As a result, they know the business inside and out. Even if the company hires someone from the outside, the person occupying the post has a ton of experience, and has been thoroughly vetted.

Therefore, shareholders can be rest assured that the combination of stable business economics and management will ensure that the company is always in good hands.

Shareholder Interest

One of the things that annoys investors the most is a management that doesn't take shareholder concerns into account when deciding on the company's future. While it's true that a share represents ownership in a business, most company managers and CEOs don't look at shareholders as their bosses.

For instance, it's hard to imagine that someone like Jeff Bezos or Mark Zuckerberg thinks that they work for their shareholders. These men have a vision and are actively working for it. As far as they're (probably) concerned, their shareholders are along with them for the ride.

Most company executives structure their shares in such a way that the shares owned by common investors have less voting rights than the ones owned by them. This way, the average shareholders don't have a say in how the company is run. If the company decides to not pay a dividend, there's not much a common shareholder can do except wait for an activist hedge fund to pick it up.

These hedge funds have the connections and power to buy shares that have significant voting rights attached to them, and can thus make a difference. However, this scenario doesn't play out with dividend stocks. The very fact that management is paying a dividend implies that they have shareholder interests at heart.

Thanks to the potential fall in stock prices if the dividend is suspended, management tends to do everything to make sure that the company earns free cash flow that is at least equal to the dividend payment. Thus, no matter what management might think or want, shareholder concerns are a priority.

While it's true that management doesn't need to ask shareholders for input into every single decision, shareholders can be rest assured that the presence of the dividend means management has to think about them when making decisions. It's a stark contrast to the way common shareholders of non-dividend-paying companies are treated.

Passive Income

Creating passive income is something that many investors dream of. Typically, the average investor's retirement plan involves saving money for a long time, building up a decent nest egg, and then investing that into something that gives them monthly cash flow. With dividend investing, investors can create passive income ahead of schedule.

What's more, it's possible to use these dividends to grow your investment at a faster rate. Thanks to dividend reinvestment programs, or DRIPs, you can reinvest your dividends back into the companies that paid you and increase your investment with them. This leads to greater dividend payments down the road, which increase both your holdings and your dividend payments.

Dividend stocks and instruments create a snowball of passive income that grows over time. What's more, if you invest in the right stocks, you could end up purchasing shares of a dividend growth company. These companies provide investors with capital gains via share price rises, and increasing cash flow thanks to increasing dividend payouts over time. You'll learn more about these companies in a later chapter.

For now, understand that passive income creation is easy with dividend investing. All you need to do is conduct a preliminary analysis of a company or opportunity, then invest your money into it. From there, DRIPs and dividend growth will ensure that your portfolio keeps increasing.

The great thing about dividend income compared to other popular income generation methods is that it's truly passive. For instance, online businesses have been touted as passive income generation machines but, those are full time businesses that you have to constantly tend to.

With dividend investing, all you do is invest your money in a stock and collect checks when you get paid. There's nothing you need to do beyond monitoring whether your investment thesis in a stock is still valid or not. If you don't want to even conduct basic stock analysis, you can invest in a fund that invests in dividend stocks for a small fee. This way, you can truly set and forget your investments and focus on things that truly matter to you. Dividend investing is versatile enough to accommodate both active and passive investors equally. No matter which approach you pick, you'll generate passive income easily.

Note that passive income generation takes time to reach significant levels. You'll learn more about this later in the book, but for now, understand that if you invest in a dividend paying ETF or mutual fund, you can expect cash flow to the tune of three percent per year from your investment. Thus, if you invest $10,000, you can expect to receive $300 per year.

$300 doesn't pay your bills or help you create financial freedom. This is why time is such an important part of passive income creation, as you have to be consistent and patient with your dividend investment strategy. Many people see numbers like this and think of them as being dismal, but they neglect to consider that their initial investment will grow over time and their dividends will increase through reinvestment.

What's more, if you keep investing money periodically into these instruments, you'll grow your portfolio considerably. For instance, let's say you invest $5,000 now, and decide to invest $500 every month for the next 30 years. Let's also assume that the market will grow at 10% per year which has been the average growth rate.

That's $1,074,211 at the end of 30 years. Assuming you want this nest egg to give you cash flow, you can invest this in instruments that pay dividends at a higher rate, say eight to 10%. These instruments won't give you capital gains, but since your objective is to generate cash flow, capital gains won't be a priority.

Thus, you'll generate cash flow of $107,421 per year, or $8,951 per month. No matter what sort of living standards you want, I'm going to hazard a guess that this amount can pay for it to a reasonable extent. This is how you build passive income over time.

In case you're wondering, none of these assumptions are out of the ordinary or unrealistic. It's possible for you to build a portfolio like this. All it takes is patience and an understanding of the value of long-term investing. It's tempting to chase instant gratification and try to time the market or jump in and out. However, doing this only hampers your ability to compound your investment. Compounding is what makes investors the most money over the long term. Make sure you have it on your side at all times by being disciplined and letting your money do the work for you.

Here is a list of historically high-yield stocks:

- US & North America

    o Roper Technologies

    o Walmart

    o Abbott Laboratories

    o Waste Connections

- - Canadian National Railway

- South America

  - Petrobras

  - BK Santander

  - Bancolombia

  - Ecopetrol

- Europe

  - Halma

  - Coloplast

  - Lindt & Sprungli

  - Diageo

- Africa

  - RMB Holdings

  - BHP Group PLC

  - Trencor LTD

- Asia & Oceania

  - BHP Group

- o Samsung Electronics

- o Softbank Corp

- o Rio Tinto LTD

Disadvantages

While investing in dividend paying instruments is great, there are a few downsides you should be aware of. For starters, while dividend stocks generate cash flow regularly, the trade-off is that you're not going to experience massive capital gains growth. This is because a company that pays dividends has likely already experienced its growth phase, and is now a large, stable company.

For example, a company like Coca-Cola isn't going to grow at 10-12% every year. It's close to impossible because their products already sell in pretty much every country on the planet. Stability and marginal growth are far more likely than exponential growth. Until someone colonizes Mars or the Moon, Coca-Cola isn't going to grow very much.

Contrast this to a company like Amazon or even Tesla. These companies are still growing, and have more markets to capture and businesses to enter. They'll need all the cash they can lay their hands on. Therefore, their stock prices will likely rise, but they're not going to pay any dividends.

As an investor, this has significant consequences for you. You can choose cash flow and stability or rapid growth and instability. Remember that a stock that has the potential to rise massively can also fall with equal speed. By investing in dividends, you're basically opting for the bird in hand rather than the two in the bush. Some investors prefer to take risks, and this approach might not sit well with them.

Another disadvantage with regards to dividend investing is that you're going to incur a tax bill. Dividends are taxed as ordinary income, which means you'll pay taxes on the payouts you receive whether you reinvest the proceeds or not. In contrast, capital gains taxes are incurred only when you sell a stock.

If you hold onto a stock forever, you'll never pay capital gains taxes and can pass them onto your heirs. You can hold onto a dividend paying stock like this, but you'll have to constantly pay taxes on the dividends themselves.

Lastly, while dividends are a great source of passive income, it takes a while before they can pay for your living expenses. You're not going to achieve instant financial freedom with them. Having said that, they're completely passive in that you don't have to do anything to earn them other than keep holding onto your stock position. As always, there's a trade-off you need to consider.

Misconceptions

To round off this chapter on the basics of dividends, let's take a look at some of the misconceptions that surround dividend investing. The biggest misconception is that dividend yields are the most important thing. A dividend paying instrument's yield is calculated by dividing the dividend payment by the price of the instrument.

For example, if a stock is selling for $10 and is paying $1 per share, its yield is (1/10) 10%. Investors look at high yields and instantly think they can earn a large amount of cash. However, there are some things to keep in mind. First, a high-yielding dividend stock isn't going to have anything in the way of capital gains.

AT&T stock is extremely popular with the high yield crowd thanks to its consistent 9-10% yield. However, look at its stock chart and you'll notice that the price hasn't moved much at all. Investors can hope for capital preservation at best. The entire benefit of holding onto AT&T stock is to earn the high yield. If you've retired, then this is an excellent investment. However, if you're younger and have some runway to grow your money, it doesn't make sense to hold onto this stock (Desjardins, 2018).

AT&T is an example of a high-quality high-yield stock, but the truth is that most high-yield stocks are terrible investments. They typically end up on high-dividend yield lists because their yield is affected both by the dividend payment as well as the price. If the price of the stock declines, the yield increases.

Obviously, if the price falls precipitously, the yield is going to skyrocket. Let's say a stock was selling for $100 the year before and paid $1 as a dividend. Its yield is one percent. If this company faces bad business conditions, its stock price will plummet. Let's say it falls to $10, which is calamitous.

However, since it hasn't made any dividend payment as yet during this year, its yield calculation will use the previous year's dividend payment and this year's stock price. Thus, the yield will be 10%. Note that this isn't a real number, and that it's just on paper. The company's losing money, and if it cannot afford to make the dividend payment, they'll slash the dividend, returning yields to their previous levels. Many new investors get seduced by high yields and end up losing a ton of money.

Another trap to watch out for is a bored or unconcerned management that uses the dividend to project an aura of safety. Here's how this racket works. Dividend stocks have a reputation of being safe. However, this isn't always the case since there's no such thing as zero risk.

Some companies' managers are majority owners of the business, and are merely using the stock market to prop their net worth's up. They drum up interest in a stock by offering to pay high dividends to investors. Ultimately, the stock price does nothing, and investors receive the dividend as a consolation prize.

In the long run, capital gains always trump dividend yields. If your time horizon is long, you should seek to maintain a balance between dividends and capital gains. This is why dividend paying growth stocks like Apple and Microsoft are so attractive since you get the best of both worlds.

In short, dividend stocks are great, but don't think of them as a guarantee of any sort. There are no such things in the market. It's best to look at them in terms of risk and their odds of success. Compared to other stock investing strategies, the odds of dividend stock investing succeeding is higher than others. This is why it makes sense to invest in them.

Chapter 2:
Investing in Dividend Stocks

Now that you know what dividends are, the obvious question is how can you get a piece of the pie? Well, the best way of investing in dividends is to buy an instrument that pays them. This means you can invest in either a stock or a fund. Investing in dividend paying stocks is riskier than investing in a fund.

For one thing, investing in a stock is a lot like buying a company. Imagine your friend runs a grocery store and approaches you for an investment. You know this person well, but no matter how deep your friendship is, you're going to want to evaluate their business prospects. You'll also ask yourself whether you know anything about the grocery business.

When it comes to investing in stocks, however, people often don't ask themselves this. Instead, they see a casino, with stock tickers replacing chips and buy/sell orders replacing bets. The results are also casino-like; some people win big, which leads to the masses thinking they can win big too. However, what happens is that they end up losing money. Before we get to how you can analyze stocks for investment, it's important for you to figure out what kind of an investor you want to be. This will inform the instruments you wish to invest in.

Investing in stocks is extremely lucrative and has the greatest reward potential. The downside is that it's a tough art to master, and most people don't succeed at it. You'll have to actively track the stocks you want to invest in and figure out how you can value these companies. This means reading annual reports and conducting a ton of research into the companies. You won't have to sit in front of a trading screen all day. However, you'll essentially be running a business, so you'll have to remain up to date with everything that is going on with the company.

Most importantly, you'll have to educate yourself in accounting and business principles. This takes time and a lot of dedication. Most people have full-time jobs, and it's questionable whether they'll have time during their day to evaluate companies like this. However, it's far from impossible. My point is that it takes a lot of hard work, and you shouldn't be misled by people who claim that they can show you shortcuts or magic ratios and those kinds of things.

Passive investing via funds is far more accessible for most people. However, the tradeoff is that your gain will be around the market average. This is why you need to remain invested for a long period of time and will need compounding to do its work, and why you won't get rich overnight. On the other hand, you can set your investing on autopilot and forget about it.

The fund manager takes care of everything, and all you'll need to do is pay a small amount as a management fee every year. That's the price you pay for building passivity into your investments. So having said all that, let's look at the instruments you can invest in.

Three Ways to Invest in Dividend Stocks

You can earn dividends by investing in instruments that pay you periodically. Every instrument is different, and payment frequencies vary. There are some that pay weekly dividends, some pay monthly, some quarterly, and so on. It's important to note that an instrument that pays dividends with greater frequency isn't necessarily better than one that pays it out over a longer period.

Some investors chase more frequent dividends for the psychological effect they have. However, this is a lot like chasing yields. It doesn't mean anything, and yields aren't affected by frequency.

Individual Stocks

Stocks that pay dividends are abundant. As you've already learned, most stocks that pay dividends are stable companies. However, it's possible to run into some poor companies that use dividends as a lure to trap gullible investors. Ultimately, you'll need to evaluate the quality of the business behind the stock before investing in it.

The best approach is to use the dividend payment as a screener and then dive deeper into a company's business. For instance, search for companies that pay dividends and then examine their financial filings in greater detail. By and large, you'll find that large companies, or so-called blue-chip stocks, pay regular dividends. These companies have names that you'll likely recognize such as Coca-Cola, AT&T, and so on (Edwards, 2021).

Some of these companies, such as Kimberley-Clark and Altria, might not be recognizable. However, their brand names, Scott Rolls and Marlboro respectively, will be. Blue chips are generally considered safe investments, but this doesn't mean they're sure things at all times; for example, Boeing is a blue-chip stock that is going through serious turmoil.

These companies can be both tough and simple to analyze at the same time. For instance, a company like ExxonMobil is one of the largest in the world, and there's no doubting its strength in weathering tough business conditions. However, given its size and depth of operations, analyzing its business is close to impossible unless you have deep connections with the management.

Therefore, a lot of investing in blue chips is done on the basis of the strength of the company's brand name. I'm not saying this is incorrect. After all, the company has invested a ton of resources into building its brand, and there's a business case to be made for investing this way. However, you must be on your toes and periodically keep checking in to make sure conditions aren't turning against the company.

Exxon is a good example of this. The world is clearly shifting away from fossil fuel, so you'd think this company is doomed to eventually go under. However, alternative energy sources haven't come close to replacing petroleum-based ones yet, and there isn't a definitive timeline of when this can happen. Besides, who's to say Exxon can't turn its ship around and begin investing in solar or wind energy farms? They'll pretty much wipe out their competition if they deploy their hefty assets in this direction.

As you can see, there's a lot of guesswork involved, which is why it's sometimes easier to stick to smaller companies. However, smaller companies usually don't pay dividends. This is where investing in dividend growth companies enters the picture.

Some of these businesses have just reached the stage where they're becoming complex but are still easy to analyze. Thus, a beginner investor can figure out what the business is about and grow with it, as opposed to looking at the finished article and trying to break down complex business units. Finding these companies is tough, but not impossible. It's a question of time and effort.

Stocks typically move in tandem with the rest of the market. This means if the market rises, they'll rise as well. If the market goes through a downturn, the stock will also fall, irrespective of how good or bad the business is. As a long-term investor, your job is to figure out what the business is worth and pay a price that is close to that value.

Stock prices and the relative value of the business are two different things. Even in everyday life, you can find such examples. For instance, let's say you walk into a grocery store and buy a bottle of water. You'll be charged five dollars for it (or $20 if you want to opt for the fruit-infused smart electrolyte spring mountain water with AI hydration chips). You're not in any hurry to buy water, and aren't thirsty. Five dollars might not match your impression of what that water is worth to you, so you might pass.

However, if you walk in when you're thirsty and really need a sip of water, you're not going to hesitate to pay that amount of cash. You might even pay more if there was such a mechanism. In the physical world, stores cannot change their prices based on demand and supply without running afoul of regulations.

In the stock market though, this happens all the time. Note that it isn't the company changing prices of stocks. Rather, other investors and short-term traders are doing so, driven by their view of supply and demand. Sometimes, you'll receive a price that is below value, and sometimes, you'll receive a price that is far above it.

Your job is to figure out what is a good price to enter the stock. If it's too high, you're free to say no and walk away. The market will always be there, so don't fall into the trap of thinking you're going to miss out. Be patient and stick to the evaluation principles I'll show you in the next chapter.

Dividend Focused Mutual Funds and ETFs

Not everyone can pick stocks successfully, which is why the market offers mutual funds and exchange traded funds (ETFs). By investing in dividend focused mutual funds or ETFs, you'll diversify your portfolio immediately with a single transaction. Mutual funds are a popular investment vehicle, but they're quite varied. Within the mutual fund world, there are two sub-categories of funds: Active and passively managed funds.

The first type of fund is called an actively-managed fund, while the second is called passively-managed. Actively-managed funds aim to beat market averages. Usually, their benchmark is the S&P 500, which is the broad market index in America. This index gives investors a snapshot of overall market performance.

Most mutual funds fail to beat this benchmark because picking winning stocks is hard. If it weren't hard enough to pick good companies, mutual fund managers have to deal with a set of constraints that make it close to impossible to make money for their clients. Every mutual fund manager has a mandate, which is a document that outlines the investment parameters to operate by.

For instance, it's not uncommon for mutual fund managers to receive a mandate that restricts them to small cap European healthcare stocks. Another condition that is imposed is to not invest more than 10% of the fund in any single stock, or that the fund manager should not invest in any company that doesn't have existing institutional presence.

These rules reduce the world of available stocks significantly. The manager cannot go out and buy AstraZeneca, or any big European healthcare sector stock, because that company isn't a small cap. Small cap refers to companies that are more than $300 million in size, up to a maximum of $2 billion. This also means that they can't buy Pfizer, because it is both an American company (not European) and a large cap (size greater than $10 billion).

Thus, mutual fund managers who manage to make money are actually performing a heroic deed. However, it's for naught as far as the small investor is concerned, because those returns do nothing for a small portfolio. You might be wondering why these restrictions exist?

Well, in short, they exist to please other financial institutions. Pension funds and managers, such as CALPERS, invest billions of dollars into different asset classes. When investing this amount of money, which is essentially ordinary people's retirement funds, they need to make sure everything is above board. Therefore, they allocate a little money to different asset classes to produce a portfolio that is conservative, but grows at a decent rate.

Investing money with a financial institution that has a number of funds with diverse mandates is the easiest way to achieve this goal. Pension fund A goes to an institution such as J.P. Morgan and tells them to allocate $10 billion across different asset classes. As a result of this, our European small cap healthcare manager receives $20 million that they have to manage according to their mandate.

Small investors lose out in this deal. Broad stock market mutual funds exist, but these funds charge high fees. Typically, you'll pay around one to two percent of your money invested as fees every year. These fees are paid whether you make or lose money. It's a significant hurdle when you take a long-term view of things.

In response to these inefficiencies, the storied financial institution Vanguard developed what's called a passive mutual fund, which is the second category of mutual fund. Instead of having fund managers pick stocks to beat the market, Vanguard's passive fund managers simply bought every stock that was present in a broad market index like the S&P 500.

After all, if the overall market was rising over the long term, surely the fund would rise too? This logic was proved correct, and these days, these passively managed index funds are a small investor's best bet. They don't charge high fees either, because a fund manager isn't picking stocks, they're merely steering the ship.

Typically, a passively managed index fund charges less than 0.1% of principal invested as fees. The average Vanguard fund, for example, charges 0.06%. Thus, index funds are a great option if you want to create a passive investment machine.

Despite their advantages, there are a few kinks in mutual funds (index funds are also mutual funds). Their prices don't fluctuate during the market day; instead, they're fixed at the end of the previous market session and remain as such until the market day ends. They're then changed to a new price for the following day.

Let's say a mutual fund has two stocks, both selling for $10 and $15. The portfolio value is $25 per unit. Now, let's say that the $15 share rises to $20. The portfolio value during the market session is now $30, but the fund is still selling for $25. In this scenario, investors are receiving more for their money.

However, what if prices decline? In that case, mutual fund investors will be paying much more than what the portfolio is worth. To fix this issue, ETFs were launched. ETFs are exactly the same as mutual funds, except their prices vary during the market session and replicate their underlying portfolio's value. This way, investors are more likely to receive fair prices. Like mutual funds, there are actively and passively managed ETFs. The passively managed ones charge lower fees and have no investment minimums, unlike index funds, so they're extremely accessible for the average investor.

How to Get Started

You can buy dividend stocks or ETFs through a broker. Brokers are a firmly established part of the financial markets, and to access the instruments you've just learned about, you'll have to go through a broker. Back in the day, brokers used to charge commissions for trading, but these days, the rise of the zero-commission broker has ensured that fees are more opaque.

It's important for you to understand that there is no such thing as zero commission, and that you'll be paying one way or another. Brokers that charge no fees make money by selling your order information to hedge funds in exchange for money. This is how brokers like Robinhood make their money. It isn't exactly a secret, they disclose it voluntarily (Kennon, 2021). While the ethics of such actions are dubious, they are legal for now.

Another thing to understand is that your broker is not your friend. No matter how much they claim to exist for the little guy or be passionate about leveling the playing field, all of it is just marketing. Your broker exists to make money off you. This is how it's always been, and will always remain the case.

Brokers in America are regulated by the Financial Regulatory Authority, or FINRA, which monitors licensing and other requirements. Many small investors think brokers are out to steal their money, but this really isn't the case. FINRA's penalties are quite harsh, and the loss of reputation is not worth it. Brokers might not be your best friend, but they're not out to baldly steal your money.

Recognize that your broker isn't there to provide financial advice. You're responsible for all the financial and investment decisions you make, so always conduct thorough research into what you're putting your money in. A broker makes money by pushing you to trade. This is how they get paid, and it's why every broker will send you trading ideas and other tempting stocks to put your money in.

Don't fall for these traps. Investing is all about keeping your money in one place for as long as possible. Your broker will get you to try and jump from one stock idea to another as if it's fashionable. However, they won't tell you that your trading activity equals commissions and fees for them. Therefore, don't do them any favors by jumping in and out of the market.

Spreads

One of the things that takes newer investors by surprise is the existence of a price spread. When you see prices on TV or on Twitter, you're often given just one price. For instance, people will say AMZN is trading at $3,500. This might lead you to think that you can buy and sell AMZN for that price.

However, the market operates on the basis of a price spread. There's a price that you'll pay when you buy and another price you'll receive when you sell. The former is called the ask, while the latter is called the bid. The difference between them is the price spread.

Price spreads aren't of huge importance to investors since you're not going to be jumping in and out of the market. However, it is of great importance to short-term traders, since they need to buy and sell at different prices and they're not looking to hold on for very long.

You should always pay attention to the spread, since it gives you an indication of what liquidity and volatility in the market are like. Liquidity is a measure of how easy some instrument is to trade. If there are many buyers and sellers in the market, then any number of shares of an instrument can be bought and sold. This makes the instrument liquid.

Volatility is a measure of the force with which prices move. The faster prices move in any direction, whether it's up, down, or both, the more volatile it is. Liquidity and volatility are often connected to one another, as low liquidity often results in high volatility. The price spread widens to reflect this, and as an investor, you're going to receive worse prices in the market.

As much as possible, avoid entering when spreads are wide. Before entering any position, watch the market for a few days to get an idea of what price spreads are like. This way, you'll know when spreads are large and can stay away from those markets.

Something else that surprises new investors is the existence of different order types. After all, isn't ordering as simple as clicking buy or sell? Well, that's what a market order is. When you place a market order, you'll receive whatever price is prevalent in the market. If the market is extremely volatile and illiquid, you're going to receive poor prices.

To mitigate this, brokers give you the option of placing a limit order. These orders have a trigger price that acts as a threshold. If you're buying an instrument, your broker will buy it at prices equal to or lower than the trigger price. When selling, your broker will sell as many shares as possible for prices that are greater than the limit price.

The catch, however, is that you're not guaranteed to receive all the shares you want. If you wanted to buy 100 shares, but your broker could only find 50 shares that satisfied the limit criteria, that's all you'll receive.

This is a problem when you're trying to exit your position.

To address this situation, a stop order type exists. These orders also have a trigger price, but your broker will focus on executing the entire order quantity once the trigger price is breached, irrespective of what the market price currently is. Generally speaking, you'll be fine placing just market orders. Limits, stops, and other order types are important to short-term traders, since they're extremely price sensitive.

Another metric to look at is Beta, a value which shows how much a stock is moving compared to the market. The idea is to look for stability when investing in dividend stocks, so you should choose ones that have low beta. When a stock's beta value is greater than one, it's more volatile than the market.

Accounts

When you first open an account with a broker, you'll have a choice of opening a margin or a cash account. To execute the dividend investing strategy, all you need is a cash account. This is the basic, default account that your broker will give you. Most brokers don't have minimum investment requirements to open cash accounts.

Brokers such as Robinhood and E-Trade allow you to open these accounts with as little as $100, but this doesn't mean you should invest as little as possible.

Simply choose a broker that doesn't have any account minimum requirements. Typically, larger brokers that are financial supermarkets will have high account minimums. There isn't any edge to be gained by investing with those brokers, so don't worry about missing out.

A margin account allows you to borrow money and stock to invest. As such, you don't need this ability, so I won't address margin account types. Before choosing a broker, make sure you evaluate their customer service and read reviews about them. Stay away from brokers that gamify the investing experience. These brokers present the market as if it's a casino and push you to gamble.

You don't need app access or mobile charts to invest well. In fact, you probably don't have to ever look at a price chart. Opt for a simple broker, and don't worry about things like options access, pre-IPO access, or the ability to buy fractional shares. You don't need any of these things to make a lot of money.

Preparing Your Investment Plan

Before you begin investing, it's important to create a plan that makes sense to you. What are your investment goals? If you're trying to implement a dividend investment strategy, then your goal is to generate enough passive income to pay for your living expenses once you retire. Depending on how many years you have left till retirement, you'll find that your dividends will either pay all or a portion of your expenses.

The way to begin is to figure out how much you realistically need per month. If you think that you'll need $5,000 per month to pay for living expenses, but are just five years out from retirement, dividend investing is not going to work for you. It takes time, and you need at least 15-20 years for best results. Ideally, you'll begin as quickly as possible.

Next, you'll need a compound interest calculator like the Investor.gov Compound Interest Calculator. Once you've fired that up, figure out how much you can contribute to your investment account every month. Let's assume you can set aside $1,000 every month for the next 25 years.

Let's also assume that the market is going to grow at a conservative eight percent every year. Plugging these numbers into the calculator gives us a total portfolio value of $877,271.28. Now, let's figure out if shifting this lump sum to a higher-yielding dividend instrument will give you enough to live on post-retirement.

Again, let's be conservative and estimate that you can generate five percent yields with this amount. This means you'll receive (0.05* 877,271.28) or $43,863 per year. This is $3,655 per month. That's a pretty good number for most people. It probably won't cover all of your living expenses, but given that you're starting from nothing, receiving that amount in 25 years every month for the rest of your life is a pretty good deal.

You can increase this monthly amount by remaining invested for longer. What if your time horizon was 30 years instead of 25? In that case, you'd have $1,359,358 at the end of that term. Assuming a five percent yield post-retirement on this lump sum, you'll receive $5,663 per month. You can see what a huge difference five more years make.

Understand that these calculations assume you'll remain invested in dividend-paying instruments throughout your lifetime. It's just that the investments pre-retirement give you capital gains as well. The ones post-retirement emphasize yield, and capital gains are secondary. It makes sense to invest in dividends before you retire as well, since the cash flow can be reinvested to produce even more gains. You'll get your wealth snowball rolling faster.

Now, it's time for you to plug your own numbers into these calculations and see what you can come up with. Always err on the side of being conservative. Use the same assumptions I've used here, and you'll arrive at a realistic retirement picture. Remember that you can boost your post-retirement cash flow by increasing the amount of money you invest per month.

How Much Cash to Invest

A common question most beginners have is to wonder how much cash they ought to invest every month. The simple answer is as much as you have, but the less simple answer is to say that you should invest all the money you have that you can afford to lose. This means you should create an emergency fund that can pay for your living expenses in case something adverse happens.

You should have enough set aside towards a home down payment, or some such expense you plan on incurring. If you plan on taking vacations every year, which is a reasonable thing to do, you must contribute to a vacation fund by setting aside enough money every month. Only after all of these expenses are accounted for should you invest money in the markets.

Some investors are unrealistic in their aims. They want the markets to pay for their down payment, or a new car or coat, etc. This is a surefire way to lose money. It makes you impatient, and you're not going to remain calm when things go against you. Markets rise and fall and then rise back up again. You'll have to weather storms all the time if you want to be successful.

Thus, only invest money that you're not going to miss. When you run the numbers for your retirement plan, play around with the monthly investment contribution you can make to arrive at your desired goals. You might find that some of these numbers might be unrealistic for you.

In such cases, aim to pay for a portion of your living expenses via passive income, or delay the date of your retirement to extend the amount of time you're invested. Always be conservative, and you'll virtually guarantee that you'll have enough cash flow to pay for your living expenses passively (Muller, 2021).

Investing Habits to Practice

Follow these investing habits to pick the best dividend stocks and funds. They'll help you avoid many of the mistakes that beginners make.

Stick to What You Know

The first principle of successful stock investment is to stick to what you know. Some investors call this the circle of competence. Whatever you decide to call it, make sure you're always sticking to companies that you can fully understand or industries that you're well-versed with.

It's a good idea to begin with companies in industries that you've worked in or are currently working in. If you've spent more than five years working for a company, chances are that you know its business pretty well, so it makes sense to begin your investment analysis with this company.

This approach is in stark contrast to the one that most investors take, where they chase the stocks that they believe are going to rise the most. They follow the financial media, whether mainstream or social, and jump from one hot stock to another. They might make money in the short term, but they're sure to lose it in the long run.

Jumping around like this increases your costs and taxes. I'll cover taxation in a later chapter, but for now, understand that short-term trading raises significant hurdles that are tough to overcome. Sticking to what you know also has another advantage, in that you'll be able to evaluate tough business conditions better.

When you invest for a long time, you will inevitably have to experience a bear market, which is when the prices of stocks decline significantly. The key to investing success is to hold on during these times and avoid selling when the market is low. Obviously, you'll need to evaluate whether the dip in prices is temporary or permanent, and this is where understanding the business comes in handy.

What's more, you'll also be able to spot potential problems before they occur. By increasing your odds of getting out at the right time, you'll end up making more money. The bottom line is that you should stick to what you know. If you feel you don't know anything about a business, or any business for that matter, educate yourself and adopt a passive investing strategy in the meantime.

Think Independently and Conduct Your Own Research

Many people blindly buy some guru's list of recommended stocks and don't take the time to critically evaluate those selections. To be a successful investor, you need to think independently and conduct your own research. The good news is that you can do this easily, since research tools and data are widely available these days.

Always form your own opinion of whether a stock is overpriced or not before buying it. Needless to say, you should always buy stocks that are underpriced. This strategy, called the margin of safety, is more of a philosophy that you should permeate everything you do.

The margin of safety is a common principle that is used in engineering. The idea is that the probabilities that go into designing a machine or a structure require engineers to estimate the value of many components.

The easiest way to ensure safety is to calculate everything and then multiply it by two. This way, the structure is almost guaranteed to be safe. Intuitively, all of us understand applying a safety margin in everything we do; if you were planning to cook for five people, you would buy food enough for more than five people to account for unforeseen events (Sullivan, 2020).

When budgeting your personal finances, you probably include a miscellaneous line item to account for expenses that you cannot foresee. In investing, the margin of safety is applied by buying a stock for a price that is lower than its value. If you think a stock is worth $50, you'll look to buy it for a price that is lower than that. This way, if the price declines, you still have a buffer to absorb downswings.

How can you figure out what a stock is worth? That's where sticking to what you know comes into play. You'll need to make some estimates of future earnings using the method I'm about to show you. However, to make those estimates, you need to know the business well enough to reasonably predict earnings.

These three investing principles will help you evaluate pretty much any prospective investment. In addition to these principles, it's important for you to learn about a few financial metrics that will help you quickly paint a picture of a company's prospects.

Play the Long Game

Price volatility is a trade-off when you're looking at capturing long term gains in common stocks. To succeed at investing, you need to think like a business owner and invest for the long term. Stocks take time to grow, which is why it's important to remain invested for a long time. As you've already seen, time is what powers compounding, and that's what makes you money.

Maintain Reasonable Expectations

The stock market isn't an overnight get-rich-quick scheme. It's meant to preserve wealth or provide moderate growth in it. Don't treat it like a casino, and expect to get rich overnight.

Stay Informed, but Don't Overmanage Portfolios

I'll address portfolio management in detail in a later chapter, but for now, remember that diving left and right trying to pick huge gainers is a losing strategy. Instead, your aim must be to own high-quality businesses that will appreciate over time. It's better to set and forget your portfolio instead of trying to always pick hot stocks.

Mistakes to Avoid When Buying Dividend Stocks

Here are the most common mistakes that people make when buying dividend stocks. Avoid these at all costs.

Buying a Stock Solely on a Hot Tip

Always do your own research before buying a stock, rather than buying something just because your friend or co-worker or some book told you to buy it. A good way to prevent yourself from falling for this mistake is to set and forget your portfolio. That way you won't feel the need to find hot stocks, since your portfolio will keep growing over time and make you money.

Not Doing The Required Research Before Buying or Selling a Stock

While buying because someone else told you to do so is a bad habit, buying without knowing anything about a stock is equally bad. To avoid this mistake, always stick to the investment habits I've outlined previously.

Focusing Solely on Yield

Yield is one of the most distracting things when looking at a dividend stock. Investors often pile into high-yielding stocks thinking they're about to earn a windfall. However, a high yield is often created due to a depressed price. If the price of a stock falls, the yield is calculated using the previous dividend payment. Since that number will be high, it results in an artificially high yield.

This means that the company might not be able to maintain that level of payments, and the investor will be left holding a stock that has no value. Focus on the underlying business at all times instead of yields.

Dismissing Stocks With Low Yields

This is a cousin of the previous mistake. Many investors who chase high yields avoid low-yielding stocks. However, the majority of low-yielding stocks tend to be stable businesses. Investors recognize the stability of the dividend payment and business prospects and buy as much stock as possible.

This results in higher stock prices and lower yields. As always, focus on the underlying business when evaluating a stock. Don't chase yields or avoid them; it's best to leave the yield out of the investment decision entirely.

Focusing on Current Rather Than Future Dividends

As an investor, you're concerned with the future prospects of your investment. Current dividend payments might look great, but as far as you're concerned, they're in the past. Make sure to evaluate the business' future prospects when making a decision, and keep in mind that larger economic effects might affect business performance.

Failing to Monitor Stocks and the Market

Set and forget is a great investment principle, but this doesn't mean you can ignore the markets altogether. You must monitor the markets for adverse events and make sure you have a plan in place to deal with them.

Don't get too caught up in the financial news, since most of it is not informational. However, monitor the basic market variables, such as the price of the S&P

500, your upcoming dividend dates, company announcements, and so on.

Buying a Stock Just Because It's Cheap

Stocks that are priced cheaply might not be great stores of value. Many investors look at a cheaply-priced stock and think they can buy a ton of shares that will increase in price, but those shares are usually cheap for a reason. The best way to avoid this mistake is to focus on the underlying quality of the business, rather than the price.

Holding a Poor-performing Stock for Too Long

While you should hold onto your investments for as long as possible, holding onto a poorly-performing stock doesn't make much sense either. You should hold onto your investment as long as you think the original investment thesis makes sense. If the stock doesn't conform to it, then you should sell it as soon as possible.

Giving Too Much Credence to Media Reports and Analysis

Mainstream financial media loves to exaggerate crises, making it seem as if everything is going to fall apart tomorrow. It's how they make money, and they often lead investors into making decisions that are bad for their financial future. Do not follow the mainstream or social media beyond checking in on basic financial information.

Failing to Account for Taxes

Keep in mind that dividends are taxable income when putting your money into them. I'll cover dividend taxation in detail in a later chapter, but remember that taxes are a key part of dividend payouts and you should always acknowledge that fact.

Failing to Reinvest Dividends

One of the best ways to supercharge compounding your wealth is to reinvest your dividends. By reinvesting your dividends via a dividend reinvestment plan (DRIP), you can buy fractional shares for no cost, and receive even more dividends the following year.

Chapter 3:
Selecting Dividend Stocks

As I mentioned in the previous chapter, you have two ways to go about selecting dividend paying instruments. The first is to actively look for stocks that pay dividends and analyze their businesses. The second is to adopt a passive approach and invest in funds that do the work for you.

Let's begin by looking at how you can make an active approach work for you.

Financial Metrics

Conducting a deep dive into accounting principles is outside the scope of this book. However, there are a few important metrics and financial statement line items that you must look at if you want to quickly identify a business' prospects. One of these ratios will help you estimate a company's value as well.

Before diving in, I'd like to note that figuring out a company's business prospects is more of an art than a science. There is no secret formula anyone can give you that will unlock a definite number that indicates what a company is worth, as it's all subjective at the end of the day. Instead of looking for definitive values, it's better to look at a ballpark figure of net worth.

This is why the margin of safety is so powerful. You cannot possibly calculate exact numbers for everything. Therefore, you need a margin of safety to account for probabilities. Always approach the question of investment as a matter of probability and you'll do just fine. This applies to both dividend-paying companies and those that don't.

Return on Equity

-Net Income/Average Shareholder's Equity

-How much the company is earning for every dollar invested.

PE Ratio

The price to earnings, or PE ratio, is often quoted in financial media. It's a useful measure of how cheap or costly a company is, relative to its earnings. It's calculated by dividing the stock price by a company's earnings per share. A high number indicates that prices are expensive, while low numbers indicate a cheap stock.

However, there are no uniform standards that indicate a cheap or expensive stock. A car company that sells for a PE of 15 is reasonable, but a tech company that sells for the same PE is ridiculously cheap. A company's stock price has estimates of future earnings built into it, and this means price and value always diverge.

For instance, high growth companies often sell for high PE ratios, with prices well above earnings. This is why companies such as Tesla, which is a tech and automaker hybrid, sells at PE ratios far greater than established automakers with a proven track record. As an investor, evaluating future prospects is your primary job.

Doing this isn't easy, which is why you need the principles you've just learned to support you. They help align the odds in your favor. The question is, how do you figure out what a company is worth numerically? You'll have to estimate future earnings to figure this out.

Let's say a company is currently earning five cents per share and is growing quickly. Over the next 10 years, you estimate that its earnings will grow by 15% on average. You can make such an estimate because you understand its business well. If its current PE ratio is 20, its stock price will be:

Stock price = Earnings per share * PE ratio = 0.05*20 = $1

In 10 years', time, its earnings will have compounded at 15% per year to give us 20 cents per share in earnings. Assuming the PE ratio remains the same, its estimated stock price in 10 years will be (.2*20), or $4. This is a 300% gain in 10 years, which is a pretty hefty return. If you assume that the PE ratio will also increase, as it often does with highly profitable companies, your estimated return increases even further.

Another way of estimating whether a stock is cheap or expensive is to flip the PE ratio around and examine it like you would any interest paying instrument. For instance, if you invest your money in a savings account, you'll receive less than one percent interest. When looking at a company, the "interest" you receive is the earnings it gives its owners. You can't claim all of this as cash, but this money goes back into the business and feeds it. In short, it's what owners get for investing money into a business.

The earnings/price ratio is essentially the same as the dividend yield formula, except we're using the full earnings amounts, not just the dividend yield. In our previous example, the stock was earning (paying) five cents per share and was selling for $1, meaning its yield is five percent.

A five percent yield indicates that the stock is quite expensive. Some investors enforce a margin of safety by buying stocks that have an earnings to price ratio of eight percent or more. It's a good way of estimating your margin of safety, but the flaw in this method is that you're not taking future growth into account.

As you just saw, this stock can provide you with a 300% return over a decade. Who cares if it's expensive? The point here is that you need to use both techniques to figure out whether a stock is a good investment or not. If you feel that a stock's future earnings are a bit unpredictable, you can build a margin of safety into your purchase price using the earnings to price method.

If you can reasonably predict future earnings, then using the earnings-to-price method is not as necessary. However, you can use it to compare how expensive a company is compared to its peers. Generally speaking, dividend paying stocks will sell for lower PEs, while growth stocks that don't pay dividends are expensive.

Dividend growth companies lie somewhere in between, and a lot depends on the sectors they're in.

Net Debt to EBITDA

-Net Debt to EBITDA

-calculated by dividing a company's total liability less cash and cash equivalents by its EBITDA

Capital Expenditures

Every business needs to reinvest its profits to grow and maintain its competitive edge. Different industries have different reinvestment needs. Some industries, such as mining and heavy industry, require significant reinvestment that can reduce profits. You've already learned about economic moats and how important they are.

One type of moat is the absence of the need to have significant capital expenditures. These businesses tend to perform better during downturns since they don't need much cash to maintain their competitiveness. This doesn't mean that every business that requires significant capital expenditure is a poor one. It's just that the odds of a low capital expenditure business performing well are high. You'll find capital expenditures listed in the statement of cash flows, under the cash from investing activities section.

There are a couple things you need to understand about the way accountants treat these expenses. For starters, they're not subtracted from revenues. For example, if a business earned $1 per share in revenue and has just $0.10 in expenses and $2 in capital expenditures, its bottom-line profit will be (1-0.1) 90 cents per share. However, capital expenditures are double revenues. The idea is that capital expenditures create assets that make money. Hence, subtracting them from revenues doesn't make sense.

From a business perspective, it's tough to figure out how to treat these expenses. A business that needs routine capital reinvestment will incur capital expenses as a regular expense. Without these expenses, the business won't make money. Therefore, subtracting them from revenues every year makes sense. Ultimately, you should look at the rest of the industry and understand the economics behind it to figure out how to treat it.

The next thing to remember about capital expenditures is that they're not subtracted from operating free cash flow. You'll learn more about this in the next subsection. For now, understand that you'll need to subtract them from operating free cash flow to get a full picture of how a company is running its operations.

Cash Flow and Income

Many beginner investors mistakenly believe that cash flow and earnings are the same thing. This isn't the case at all, as a company's income or profits are listed in the income statement's final line, hence the term bottom-line earnings. Cash flow is listed in the cash flow statement.

A company's earnings can be manipulated pretty easily. There are many non-cash expenses that are subtracted from revenues to calculate earnings. In addition to this, the way some expenses are categorized don't make sense for every industry. For example, depreciation is a notoriously fudged expense.

Let's say you buy a piece of furniture and hang onto it for 10 years. You've paid a certain amount of cash to purchase it, making it an expense. Since furniture is an asset, the expense is a capital expenditure. Now, the question arises: What is it worth in the third year of ownership? How can you estimate its value?

The only way you can figure out this value is by selling the furniture. However, why would you sell it just to figure out its price? You'll sell it when you want to get rid of it. Recording the value of an asset is all-important since it goes on a company's balance sheet.

To deal with this issue, accountants assume that the value of that piece of furniture will decrease, or depreciate, by a fixed percentage every year, usually at 10%. At the end of 10 years, that asset will be worth close to nothing on a company's books. The problem here is that the rate of depreciation can be changed. Reputable accountants won't do this, but there are many companies that routinely change depreciation rates. If the depreciation rate is increased, the depreciation expense increases, and profits decrease. If the rate is decreased, expenses decrease, and profits increase.

The other thing to note is that depreciation isn't a cash expense. It has no impact on the amount of money in a company's bank account, so earnings don't equal cash. The cash flow statement gives investors a clear picture of cash in a company and adds back depreciation and other non-cash expenses. However, capital expenditures are not subtracted from cash flow from operations. The bottom line of the cash flow statement shows the free cash flow, which takes everything into account.

The problem is that this number also takes cash raised from issuing equity or debt into account. If a company loses cash from its operations, then loses even more due to capital expenditures, but raises enough cash by issuing shares in the market to cover these holes, it will have a positive free cash flow.

However, from an investor's perspective, this is hardly a good situation. A company that cannot make money from its primary activity isn't a good business to invest in. Ideally, you should consider the number you receive by subtracting capital expenditures from the cash flow from operations. That number will give you a good idea of how well the business generates cash.

At the end of the day, you should only take this number into account since it represents real earnings. You could even use it to calculate the PE ratio by using this number instead of earnings.

Debt-to-Equity Ratio

The debt-to-equity ratio tells you how volatile you can expect a company's stock to be. It's not a direct measure, as different industries have different standards, but it gives you a good idea of the risk you're undertaking by investing in the company. Generally speaking, you want debt to be lower than equity. However, this reduces the chances of a sharp rise in stock prices.

Equity is what shareholders own and debt is what creditors own. Let's say you control an asset that is worth $100. You own $1 while you've borrowed $99. In this case, $1 is equity, while $99 is debt. Now, let's say that the price of this asset increases to $101. Its price has increased by just a dollar, but you've realized a gain of 100% on equity.

The flip side is that if it decreases by a dollar, you'll have lost all of your equity. A high amount of debt boosts your gains, but it cuts the other way as well, and can bankrupt you quickly if you're not careful. The same phenomenon occurs with companies; high debt levels create volatility in stock prices, but if a company has poor results, stock prices can nosedive quickly.

There's also the cash burden that excessive debt places on companies. If a company doesn't make its interest payments on time, its assets will likely be seized by creditors. High debt levels are thus a double-edged sword that cuts both ways. Usually, dividend-paying companies don't have huge debt levels. This is one of the reasons why they remain stable for long periods of time, and don't experience the rapid growth in stock prices that highly-leveraged companies do.

Monitor debt levels closely to make sure the company isn't borrowing too much money. If things go bad and you notice that the company needs to borrow money to pay its dividend, that's about as bad things can get. This is because a company that needs to pay off its debt will pull those resources away from paying dividends; if the ratio gets high enough, you should exit your position immediately, no matter how high the dividend is.

While excessive debt is bad, you don't want to invest in a company that has zero debt either. This indicates the company repeatedly issues stock to raise capital, which is a bad thing for existing shareholders. Imagine a pizza pie being repeatedly cut into smaller portions. That's what repeated stock issues do to existing investors. Their piece of the pie decreases, and there's no point remaining invested for the long term (Tahiri, 2019).

Payout Ratio

The payout ratio is a metric that is specific to dividend paying companies, calculated by dividing the amount of dividends paid by the total earnings. Again, like with other metrics, there isn't a fixed number that indicates a good payout ratio. Obviously, the lower it is, the better. However, a high number doesn't necessarily indicate weakness.

A lot of this metric depends on the industry. For example, utility companies payout a large proportion of their earnings to investors because their businesses are stable and highly regulated. As such, they don't have much use for the majority of the cash they generate. Therefore, it makes sense for them to payout 60% or more of their earnings.

However, if the likes of Microsoft starts paying out more than 40%, alarm bells should start ringing. The technology sector is highly competitive, and large payout ratios indicate decreasing earnings since companies automatically hang onto their cash to ward off competitors.

Always compare payout ratios across companies in an industry to get a sense of what's sustainable. If you can't find a decent standard, then calculate the payout ratio using free cash flow from operations, less capital expenditures. This will give you a clear picture of how sustainable the dividend is. A high value in this ratio indicates possible issues within the company.

Key Dividend Ratios To Know

There are a few dividend-specific ratios you ought to know before investing in dividend stocks. The first is a relatively straightforward one called the dividend per share, which is the amount of money paid as dividends per share. A growing dividend per share is a good sign when looking at a company. The next metric is the dividend yield, which is calculated by dividing the dividend paid per share by the share price. It's one of the most misunderstood metrics out there, since many investors think it's the only one that matters.

As I've explained previously, a high yield doesn't guarantee a good investment, as it can be created by a tumbling stock price. As a rule of thumb, anything greater than four percent yield is unsustainable and deserves a closer look. Look for signs of excessive debt or earnings that cannot be sustained according to the metrics we've already discussed.

The dividend payout ratio is another important metric, as it measures how much of a company's net income goes towards making dividend payments. Generally speaking, 80% of net income paid as dividends and above are unsustainable. Remember that the net income can be fudged via depreciation, as I've previously explained. Some investors choose to calculate the payout ratio using the company's free cash flow instead.

The dividend growth rate measures the rate at which a company has been increasing its payouts. It's a handy measure of how well a company has been growing its payouts to investors. Lastly, we have the dividend coverage ratio, which measures how much the net income covers the dividend payment. It's quite similar to the payout ratio, and some investors choose to measure the free cash flow coverage instead.

Profit margins

-The key to look for is a steady or increasing profit margin. When you see that, dividend payments are likely to continue and even rise.

Current ratio

-the ratio between the company's liquid assets and short-term debt obligations

-Companies with a current ratio above 1.5 are most likely to spread their wealth with investors

Earnings per share

-Profit divided by outstanding shares of common stock

-The higher the EPS, the more profitable

Company age

-Consider companies that have been public for at least 10 years. This way you have plenty of data to base your decisions on

Growth expectations

-seek out companies with long-term profitability and earnings growth expectations between 5% and 15%.

Industry/Sector trends

-look at the broader sector, to cultivate a more holistic projection of future performance.

How do I Know if I'm Paying Too Much, or if It's A Good Price?

The easiest way to evaluate price is to look at the following metrics.

Price-to-Book Ratio

This is the value of the company's market price per share divided by the book value per share. If you find that the P/B ratio is low, it's a sign that the company is undervalued.

Another ratio you can use is the PE ratio, which I've previously discussed. The company's free cash flow per share is also a good way of measuring what you're getting for the price you're paying per share.

Forward Dividend

This metric is also called the forward dividend yield. Wall Street analysts are a smart bunch, and they project the potential dividends that a company can be expected to earn in the future with high accuracy. Dividing these payments by the current price gives us the forward dividend yield. Make sure to look for stocks with a forward dividend yield greater than the current yield.

Industries

The following sectors are great sources of finding potential dividend paying stocks.

- Utilities: Electricity, water, and natural gas suppliers are great sources of dividends since their industries are highly regulated and there's a high barrier to competition. Their revenues are also assured because these products are essential and people always need them. The downside is that growth is limited due to regulation, but if steady cash flow is your aim, utilities are a good bet.

- Energy: Energy companies frequently create master limited partnerships, called MLPs, that I'll explain in more detail later in this book. These companies offer tax advantages and steady dividend payments.

- Telecommunications: These companies fall under the utilities bracket, even if their sectors are different, and thus offer the same advantages. Business is assured and dividend cash flow is secure.

- Consumer Staples: Sticking with the theme of products that every consumer requires, consumer staples such as food, beverages, and consumer products etc are steady sources of dividend payments.

- Real estate: Real estate investment trusts (REITs) are great sources of income. I'll describe them in detail later in this book.

Types of Dividend Stocks

There are many companies that pay a dividend in the stock market, and all of them have been classified into categories to make it easy for investors to figure out how reliable they are. There are three broad categories of companies that indicate the sustainability of their dividend.

Dividend Kings

These stocks are the best of the best when it comes to dividend payments. These companies have not only maintained their payments for over 50 years, but they've also increased their dividend payments during that time. Companies like Coca-Cola are a part of this list.

These companies are extremely stable and you can count on increasing dividend checks from them. The problem is that there isn't much capital growth in these companies, since they're so large that there isn't much room for them to grow anymore.

There's also a danger that they might get disrupted by newer competition due to inertia. All of these companies are old guards of the American economy, and thus, inertia is likely to ruin them. Having said that, there has never been an instance of a Dividend King going bankrupt. The combination of having lasted for over 50 years and paying a steady dividend means the company is as close to bulletproof as possible.

Dividend Aristocrats

While the Kings have maintained a steadily increasing dividend for over 50 years, the Aristocrats have done so for 25 years. This list is filled with Kings and a few other companies. While it's not as impressive as maintaining an increasing dividend for 50 years, 25 years is nothing to sneeze at.

Like with the Kings, you can't expect outsized capital gains with these companies. They tend to perform to market average levels in the long run, which makes them a safe investment. However, if you have some time to go before retirement, you might want to consider an investment that offers the promise of greater capital gains.

This is something that escapes most dividend investors. While dividend yields are great, they don't create anywhere near as much wealth as capital gains do. This is why prioritizing capital gains over long investment horizons is a better approach. I'm not saying you ought to ignore dividends, but you should use them as a sign of stability instead. Don't prioritize them until you need your portfolio to generate cash for passive income that can pay your living expenses.

Dividend Achievers

The Achievers are companies that have maintained steady dividend increases for at least 10 years. These companies are still growing, but not as fast as an early-stage company. However, having the potential to grow more makes them a good choice for investors looking for the safety of dividend payments and the potential of capital growth.

Microsoft and Costco are prime examples of such companies. If your investment horizon is more than 15 years, then investing in these companies is a great way to build your portfolio (Edwards, 2021).

Tips in Choosing Stocks to Start With

The best place to start is with the Dividend Aristocrats and then apply the following criteria:

- PE ratio less than 20

- Dividend yield less than 2.5%

- Payout ratio less than 75%

- Earnings per share over the next five years should be positive

There are a variety of free and paid tools that give you most information on a stock that you need. Stock screeners in brokerage accounts also offer these to help you narrow down your stock picks based on a certain criteria, and many individual stock brokerage accounts also provide online research and pricing information and ratios to their customers. Financial news sites and apps such as CNBC, Morning Star, and Yahoo! Finance are also a useful resource. Dividend.com also offers lists of stocks to choose from, as well as a watchlist tool.

Fund Issuer

The issuer of a passive fund is extremely important, since in this arena, size matters. The larger and more reputed an institution is, the lower their fees and trading costs. Larger institutions will have been around for longer, and will have a more stable management team.

Vanguard is the largest fund issuer on the market. acting as the pioneer. Their fees are consistently the lowest, and it's hard to go wrong with their funds. Other issuers, such as Charles Schwab, J.P. Morgan Chase, iShares, Fidelity, and Nuveen Asset Management, are also reputable companies.

This isn't an exhaustive list by any means, as there are a large number of stable fund issuers. If you're unsure of an issuer's reputation, then take a look at their fees. Smaller fund issuers charge greater fees.

Fund Size

The size of a fund determines the fees they'll be charged by their brokers. Fund size is also a proxy for figuring out investor confidence in the fund's management. Typically, it's best to stick to funds that are larger than $5 billion in size, whether they're index funds or ETFs. You'll find that funds of this size will have less volatile performance. The reason smaller funds have volatility issues is because their investors routinely move money in and out of the fund. As fund size changes, so does the portfolio size, so the manager has to constantly rebalance their portfolio to match the weights in the index.

For instance, if the portfolio size is $100 million and stock A is weighted at three percent in the index, the position size of A in the fund's portfolio must be $3 million. If the fund's size increases to $200 million, thanks to new money flowing in, stock A must now be $6 million, meaning the manager has to buy a lot more stock and incur fees. Meanwhile, if investors pull money out of the fund, thereby reducing its value to $150 million, the manager has to rebalance once more.

These trading costs are passed onto the investor and performance suffers, so stick to large funds that have both lower costs but less capital flows. Stability comes with size, as do lesser trading fees.

Lag

All index funds lag their indexes due to trading costs. The trick is to minimize this gap, and funds have creative ways of doing this. Some funds expand the scope of their indexes to include companies that satisfy index criteria, but aren't included in the index.

For example, Tesla is currently one of the 500 largest companies by market cap in America. However, it isn't present in the S&P 500. Fund managers looking to replicate the S&P 500 and minimize the gap to the index might buy Tesla and capture additional performance from that stock to cover the gap. This means that there is some discretion that the fund manager has on the portfolio.

Discretion is a good thing because you don't want a robot managing your portfolio (given the current state of robots). However, giving a manager discretion can go wrong, since they could turn the fund into a quasi-market beating fund that increases the chances of things going sour.

You want to see a balance in the way the fund manager runs things. Fees are a direct window into this. Funds with higher fees offer their managers more discretion, and their portfolios are typically more aggressive. If your aim is to capture passive market gains, it makes sense to simply choose the fund that has the lowest expense ratio (annual fees charged divided by portfolio value) and the lowest performance lag.

You'll have to look at the combination of these two values and match them to your risk appetite. For example, let's say we have funds A and B as below:

- Fund A: Performance lag -0.2% and expense ratio - 0.06%
- Fund B: Performance lag -0.1% and expense ratio -0.07%

B lags less, but that's eliminated by its higher expense ratio. Thus, there isn't a difference between these funds. Choose the less expensive combination while looking at rewards via lower lag at all times.

Fund Manager

The fund manager isn't as important with a passive fund as they are with an active fund. However, you don't want someone incompetent in charge. Ideally, this person will be risk-averse and won't have any ideas about trying to dominate the markets. Stability is an important issue, and you should always view performance historically.

Larger funds have been around for a while and have gone through managerial change. Look at when the managers changed and check to see whether fund performance changed with it. The more stable the return profile is, the better.

Something to look at is whether the fund manager likes moving the goalposts. This doesn't happen much with the large funds, but smaller funds tend to do this quite a lot. The reason this happens is because the manager creates an investment goal by picking an index to follow. They then discover that it's a bad choice, and change the fund's strategy by picking another index.

For example, a number of funds that invest in Chinese technology companies have done this over the past few years. Many funds have arbitrarily changed their index goals to capture market performance of companies that are not government-owned in the tech sector.

Why would government ownership be such a huge factor? More importantly, doesn't government ownership in a communist country guarantee more stability? Watch out for such weird changes in goals. Typically, it happens because the fund manager is trying to beat the market by picking exotic indexes that have no relevance to anything.

Chapter 4:
Investing Strategies by Investment Goal

There are several different approaches that dividend investors can take, depending on their investing goals. In this section, I'll discuss the main ones.

Dividend Growth Approach

This approach is a classic combination of buying stocks that have a high growth rate, but are also paying a good amount of dividends per share. The idea is to buy a stock that currently might be paying a low dividend, but thanks to the capital gains increases, will begin paying a greater yield in the future.

Long-term owners of such stocks expect them to grow significantly, which justifies the lower dividend yield. Eventually, when the company has expanded to a certain size, it will begin paying more dividends, since growth at that stage will be slower. Dividend growth stocks have outperformed the market from 1972 until 2014, with far lower volatility.

It's best to choose companies that have strong competitive advantages or moats. From a portfolio perspective, it's best to hang onto these companies for a long time, even decades, to take advantage of deferred capital gains taxes. It's also a good idea to diversify across many industries, since that ensures your portfolio isn't reliant on a single sector of the economy.

Make sure the dividend growth is being financed by earnings, rather than by debt. Examining the ratios, I listed in the previous chapter will help you do this easily. It's even better to own dividend stocks listed in multiple currencies from multiple countries, meaning that you're not dependent on a single government or currency to earn dividends.

High Dividend Yield Approach

This is a conventional passive investing strategy in which the idea is to capture the highest dividend yield possible without sacrificing safety. This strategy is best for investors who are looking to capture as much cash flow as possible.

Typically, the companies that this strategy yields are slow growth companies, because the majority of their earnings tend to be diverted towards dividends instead of retained earnings. Stocks in defense sectors, pharma, food, housing, and utilities tend to adhere to these qualities.

Remember that this strategy won't yield the highest capital gains, since dividend growth companies tend to beat high-yield companies over the long term.

Year	3% initial yield + 10% annual dividend growth	7% initial yield + 3% annual growth
1	$300	$700
5	$489.14	$1,024.87
10	$901.21	$1,650.56
15	$1,660.43	$2,658.25
20	$3,059.23	$4,281.14
25	$5,636.43	$6,894.81
30	$10,384.75	$11,104.17
35	$19,133.23	$17,883.37
40	$35,251.74	$28,801.34
45	$64,949.04	$46,384.85
50	$119,664.40	$74,703.27

As you can see, the high-yield stock has a head start, but it is eventually beaten by the high-growth stock.

Broad-Based Index Approach

This is a middle of the road approach where you want dividends, but admit that you don't know much about evaluating individual companies. For example, you could buy an index fund that tracks the S&P 500 because you believe that the U.S economy will grow over the long term.

The biggest risk with this approach is the future of earnings growth. Investors can either be optimistic or pessimistic depending on the type of growth they've priced in, and markets can fluctuate because of these estimates.

Another risk is that you might end up investing in companies you don't morally find tasteful. For instance, you could end up investing in tobacco companies or oil companies. You'll never beat the market with these broad-based funds, but it's a good way to capture market average performance.

Dividend Capture Approach

This is an active strategy that will require you to trade and monitor the markets a lot. The idea is to buy the stock just before the ex-dividend date and sell it to capture the dividend payment. This strategy is not recommended for the average investor, since the risks are high; the potential for losses is high, while the profits are low.

This approach requires you to constantly bag winners, which can be tough given how random the markets are. However, if you can pull it off, it's a steady income earner and you don't have to own dividends for the long term.

Take note that brokerage commissions (brokers catering to short term traders charge them) and taxes will eat into your gains. It's best to do your homework before deciding to adopt this approach.

Chapter 5:
Investing Methods

There are multiple ways you can scale into the stocks you wish to buy as part of your portfolio. In this chapter, I'll cover the most important ones.

Dollar Cost Averaging

This is a no-brainer investing method that you can follow regardless of market conditions. The idea is to invest a fixed sum of money in the market at regular intervals. If you have a lump sum of money to invest, you'll break that into equal amounts and invest all of it piecemeal.

The advantage of this method is that you can avoid the shock of investing a large sum and seeing the market drop. By spreading out your investment, you'll be riding the ups and downs of the market better.

If the market drops, your investment is low and you'll be able to buy more shares. If the market rises, your previous investments will make money and you'll buy less shares with your new contribution, thereby avoiding buying at the top. Dollar cost averaging is a long-term strategy regardless of how much you want to invest, and the key is to keep investing at a regular interval at all times.

The disadvantage of this method is you'll likely miss out on massive gains in the market. For instance, if you bought $100 worth of an ETF at $50 per share, you'll be buying just two shares. If its price rises to $200, you'll be earning a profit of $300 ($150 per share). If you had bought $5,000 worth of the ETF, your gains would have been much larger. The flip side is that if the price of the ETF declined, you would have lost a lot of money, which is avoided since you've invested just $100.

Dollar cost averaging is pretty simple to execute. Let's say you begin buying an ETF in January in amounts of $100 and its price is $50, starting off with two shares. In February, you'll invest $100 again, but let's assume the ETF's price rises to $100. In this month, you'll buy just one share. Thanks to the repeated purchases of the same amount over the year, the number of shares of the ETF will slowly increase, while your average cost price will change in line with the ETFs price movements.

Value Averaging

This method is an improvement on dollar cost averaging, but it's trickier to get right. The idea behind value averaging is to buy more shares when prices decline and to buy less when prices are up. The problem, however, is figuring out which prices qualify as the ETF being "up" and which ones qualify as being "down".

A simple way to combat this problem is to compare prices to your last purchase. Like with dollar cost averaging, you'll buy fixed amounts of stock at regular intervals. However, if the price of the stock rises since you last bought it, you'll buy less of it.

Let's say you buy an ETF in January for $50, investing $100 into it and netting you two shares. Now, let's assume that in February, its price declines to $25. Under dollar cost averaging rules, you would have bought $100 worth of stock again, resulting in four shares.

However, you'll double your investment under value averaging rules instead since the price has declined by half. Thus, you'll invest $200 (instead of $100) and buy eight shares. If the price had risen to $100, you would have invested $50 since the price doubled. In reality, you wouldn't have been able to place an order to buy units of the fund unless your broker allows you to buy fractional shares.

Over time, you'll end up buying more shares during downturns and less during upturns. This has the effect of lowering your cost price dramatically, and the profits you'll earn will be greater than with dollar cost averaging. Psychologically, it's a tougher strategy to execute since you'll have to remain on the sidelines when the market rises.

Another potential downside is that an investor might run out of money in a down market due to investing larger amounts of money. As the market keeps declining, the investor will have to keep investing ever increasing amounts to stick to this strategy. However, it's a great strategy in the long run, since your average cost will be low.

Buying Only the Dips

This strategy involves buying only when the target stock or mutual fund drops or takes a dip in value. It can provide better returns than a dollar cost averaging strategy, but you need to follow your target stocks or funds to make investments when the valuations have dropped. This strategy potentially requires the investor to time their lump sum and periodic investments while waiting for a more favorable price.

Psychologically, it's once again a tough strategy to follow because you'll remain on the sidelines when the price is rising. As everyone is jumping into the market, you'll have to remain on the sidelines and watch as the prices rise without acting. However, discipline will pay off and you'll end up buying at lower prices.

Lump Sum

Lump sum strategies are the simplest to follow, since all you need to do is invest a large amount into the market whenever you have the money. The sums you invest don't need to be the same, as you simply need to invest everything you have. If you invest into the market fully according to the guidelines you've learned so far, you'll manage to grow your portfolio considerably.

The lump sum strategy will give you good returns if the market is rising, but if it drops, there is the risk of being stuck with poor investments for longer. If the stocks you're investing in pay good dividends, then the lump sum strategy will offer better returns than the dollar cost averaging method.

Investment Plans

There are different ways you can build your portfolio and add to your dividend stocks. Here are some of them.

Fixed Investment + Reinvesting Dividends

This plan entails you investing a fixed amount of cash and fully reinvesting your dividends via a DRIP. As previously mentioned, DRIP stands for dividend reinvestment plan, and it's something that your broker will offer for free. There are many advantages to DRIPs, such as buying fractional shares in your stock or fund for zero charges. Most brokers don't offer the ability to buy fractional shares with a new investment, but all of them allow you to do so via a DRIP.

This means you can compound your dividends over the long term, since your investment in the fund keeps increasing. It'll be slow going at first, but you'll notice that your dividends end up contributing significantly to your overall investment over time.

Something to note is that DRIPs don't absolve you from taxes on your dividend investment. Many investors forget this, since they don't see their dividends come in as cash. Your broker will automatically reinvest the money, so it can be easy to forget that you owe taxes on them at the end of the year. Some investors don't like DRIPs for this reason since it's a cash outflow during tax time. However, the long-term benefits of a DRIP greatly outweigh the negatives.

Regular Top-Up + Reinvesting Dividends

This plan entails you investing a certain amount of cash at regular intervals and fully reinvesting your dividends via a DRIP. Your top-up investment amounts should be determined before you enter the market. Consistency is important, so make sure you choose an amount that you can stick to and successfully invest over a long period of time, even if it's only $100. Consistency is what makes money in the market, and you don't want to overcommit and end up missing out in potential gains.

As I mentioned previously, the downsides of regular, fixed investments will make themselves known. It's important for you to figure out what works best and then follow that strategy.

Same Stock Reinvesting Plan

In this plan, you'll be investing whatever money you have into your existing portfolio as much as possible, while withdrawing your dividends. This means you'll receive a cash balance at whatever intervals your stocks pay you dividends in, and that you'll have to decide what to do with your cash.

If your aim is to reinvest it, you can simply choose a DRIP. However, if the cash you're receiving is substantial enough, then you can choose to redirect this money into new investments that offer potentially greater returns. This is a great way of boosting your investments and having your existing stocks pay for new ones. It's also a suitable plan for those nearing retirement since cash flow becomes more important as you near retirement age.

Reinvesting in Higher-Yielding Stocks

This investment plan is great for boosting cash flow. The idea is that you reinvest the dividends you receive into stocks that pay a high dividend. You'll increase the amount of cash you receive, while allocating your initial investments to the stocks or funds you first chose.

For example, let's say you invested in an ETF and plan to allocate regular sums of $100 every month to it. Whatever dividends it pays you can be directed towards a high yield dividend-paying stock. Let's say you invest in AT&T stock, which yields 10%. The dividends you invest in AT&T will increase your cash flow, and you can either reinvest those into the high-yielding stock or redirect them to the ETF.

Meanwhile, your regular investment amount keeps going into the ETF, boosting your dividend cash flow even more. It's a bit risky constructing a portfolio like this, but if you can pull it off, you'll compound your gains a lot faster.

Chapter 6:
Building and Managing Your Portfolio

Building a portfolio is an important skill for any investor to have, because a strong portfolio will guard you from market downturns and adverse events. You can expect these events to occur over a long enough timeline, and portfolio management will help you sail through these storms

Portfolio Best Practices

Once you've figured out your ideal strategy and have committed to following the best way of building your portfolio, you should focus on executing the following best practices.

Put Cash to Work

Active investors will run into situations where they have cash lying around waiting to be invested, but there are no suitable opportunities. The stock they're looking to buy might be too expensive, or there might not be any good companies to buy. During such times, invest your money in a liquid interest-bearing account, like a savings account, and wait for the right opportunity.

While the interest you earn won't be much, the point isn't to earn interest. Instead, it's to manage your cash balance and keep it ready when opportunity knocks. Don't be in a rush to invest it in a less than high-quality stock. If you always stick to the investment principles you've learned thus far, you'll be fine.

Monitor Your Investments

The degree to which you monitor your portfolio depends on your investment strategy. Active investors will need to track their holdings more than passive investors. Having said that, there's no need for active investors to track stock prices once they've bought them. Instead, you should track company filings and other related news releases, since you need to check whether your investment thesis is still relevant.

Passive investors should read the annual fund prospectus to make sure there aren't any changes in the fee structure or strategy that could jeopardize the market average goal they're trying to achieve.

At the end of the day, portfolio construction is an important skill that every investor must learn. Thankfully, it isn't too tough to get right. Stay away from nonsensical treatises about buying 30 stocks across every sector of the stock market and so on. Keep it simple, and you'll be just fine.

Building up Your Portfolio

The first thing to realize is that at first your portfolio will produce small amounts of dividend income. This is because your investment amounts will be low, and the dividend amounts won't be much. For example, if you invest $5,000 into a dividend portfolio that yields three percent, you'll receive $150 per year in dividends. That doesn't really sound like much, does it?

However, if you've invested in dividend growth stocks, your dividend amounts will increase over time as the stock prices rise. If the companies in your portfolio increase their dividends by six percent per year (which is a conservative estimate), you'll be earning $269 per year within 10 years. All of this comes without investing any additional money or reinvesting dividends.

My point is that you need to give your money time to compound, because that's what creates a money snowball that increases itself over time. Keep reinvesting your dividends and keep investing money at regular intervals; you'll manage to automatically grow your portfolio over time, and your dividends will increase.

The key is to remain invested over long periods of time. That's what powers compounding, and what ensures that your money grows optimally over the long run.

Your Portfolio Size

The first step to building your portfolio is to figure out how much dividend income you'd like from your stocks. Let's say you want $40,000 in income per year, and you're comfortable with a basket of stocks that yield five percent. Remember that you'll have to account for taxes as well.

Next, multiply the income (40,000) by 1.25 to cover taxes and then divide this number by the yield to give you your ideal portfolio size. This calculation results in a portfolio value of $1 million. Remember that there's a time element to this calculation, and that you don't have to generate this amount of money right now. Building up to it is the key.

After this, start picking your stocks and aim for the desired yield you would like. Pick from a spectrum of dividend yield and dividend growth stocks to hit your goal. Over time, your portfolio will grow and you'll manage to hit your goal.

Risk Management

No portfolio is immune to market movements, whether up or down. This is why risk management is so important. The goal of your portfolio is to produce a steady income stream, which is why diversification is essential. A concentrated portfolio is risky since you'll be depending only on a few stocks.

Always conduct thorough due diligence before you invest. Don't let emotions dictate your investment choices, and be especially careful of greed, fear, and love.

Setting up Your Portfolio

It's best to diversify your holdings to at least 25 to 30 stocks. Ideally, the weight of these positions in your portfolio should be equal. Don't invest in more stocks than this number, because it can be tough to keep up with them.

It's also important to diversify your money across five to seven industries, since stocks from similar industries are more susceptible to market forces operating in those sectors. You don't want your portfolio to decline because of a single sector's low performance. Pick sectors that are non-correlated with one another so that a single sector's performance doesn't affect another's.

Always use common sense when you're looking to diversify, and stick to the areas of the market that you know.

Recommendation for Allocations for Each Stock

There are various ways to allocate your money in your portfolio. First, you should diversify through market cap. There are enough large cap companies that pay dividends for you to build a diversified portfolio. Owning even three large cap stocks will give you the mutual fund effect, allowing you to replicate their amazing performance via a diversified portfolio. Be sure to focus on large caps before getting into medium and small caps.

In addition to owning blue chip American stocks, it's prudent to also own a few international stocks in order to diversify your location risk. Geographic diversification will help you eliminate a lot of political risk.

Have more weight in Consumer Non-Cyclical Food and Beverage/ Basic Needs or healthcare industries

If you have a larger portfolio ($25000 and up), you can include some other sectors such as Industry (aerospace, machinery, waste management), or regulated utility.

Reinvesting Dividends

Always reinvest your dividends via a DRIP, since this allows you to increase your investment and multiply your returns without any effort. Additionally, you can also buy fractional shares as I've already explained and grow your portfolio that way.

Monitoring and Rebalancing

It's best to keep an eye on how your stocks are performing at least once every quarter or year; after all, companies are not obliged to pay dividends, and can raise or slash them at any time. Make sure your dividends are being issued regularly, and that the amount is growing. Always check to make sure your investment is growing, and don't tolerate any declines in performance.

A few metrics to keep track of include the income your portfolio is generating, the safety with which this income is being generated, the degree with which you're diversified, and whether you need to readjust your allocations.

When rebalancing, check to see if any stocks in your portfolio have deviated from your preferred allocation percentages. It's best to set up percentage triggers at specific dates in the calendar year that will notify you that you need to rebalance your portfolio. Remember that you don't always have to sell to rebalance, as you can add funds to achieve target allocations too.

In addition to portfolio rebalancing, you must also rebalance within a sector to make sure your allocations are ideal. If you own six companies in the same sector, your allocations might deviate from the ideal, so make sure you rebalance between them.

During a Recession

Markets crash from time to time, and it's important for you to handle these events well. It's important that you liquidate your losers, selling those companies whose prospects are bad and allocate that money to companies who are expected to do well. Another option is to sit on your cash and wait for better opportunities to arrive.

Rebalance your portfolio towards those stocks that are poised to thrive during recessions. These stocks will probably give you a high yield as well since all stock prices generally decline during these times.

When to Sell a Dividend Stock

Watch out for these signs in the stocks in your portfolio. If any of them occur, it's probably a good idea to sell them.

1. Declining cash flow: This indicates that the company is in trouble and it might not be able to meet its dividend requirements.

2. Credit downgrade: A company's credit rating is its lifeline since it defines how much money it can raise from banks. A low credit rating puts pressure on cash flow, which could affect the dividend.

3. Weak fundamentals: Monitor the metrics I previously listed to ensure that a company's performance is good.

4. Long term impairment to earning power: The metrics I previously spoke about will clue you in as to whether a company can maintain its earning power or not. Sell when there's danger to its ability to generate money.

5. Suspended stock buyback programs: A company needs cash to buy back its stock, and if it suspends this program, it means its cash position is in trouble.

6. Falling stock price and rising yield: A rising yield created by falling stock prices is a false yield,

acting as a dividend trap. Stay away from such companies.

7. Stock's valuation has reached excessive levels: Stocks often become overvalued in the market, and it makes no sense to buy them at those prices. Use the PE and PB ratio to figure out when stocks are overvalued.

8. Portfolio weight increase: A stock will occasionally reach an uncomfortable level of weight in your portfolio. During these times, it's best to sell and rebalance your portfolio away from that stock.

9. Better investment opportunities: If you find another stock that is going to give you better returns, then sell your existing holdings and buy that stock instead. Always be on the lookout for better opportunities, and jump into new stocks that give you better growth prospects.

10. Dividend safety is compromised: If you think the safety of the dividend is compromised, it's best to exit the position immediately.

Above all else, do not decide to buy or sell based on your emotions.

Chapter 7:
Taxes and Dividends

Dividend taxation can get a bit complicated, but it isn't too hard to figure out. You'll need to learn this stuff because you will incur an additional tax burden. The good news is that almost everything is taken care of for you by your broker. However, you still have to file your taxes at the end of the fiscal year, so it's worth learning how taxation of dividends works.

Qualified Versus Ordinary

There are two types of dividends that a company can pay you. The first is a qualified dividend, and the second is an ordinary one. There are a few misconceptions surrounding qualified dividends, so let's clear them up.

Firstly, the company decides whether a qualified dividend, or a portion of it, is qualified or not. Secondly, your holding period determines whether you can access the benefits provided by qualified dividends. To qualify, you must have held the stock for more than 60 days during the prior 181-day period before the ex-dividend date. If these two conditions are met, the dividend is qualified.

The benefit that qualified dividends receive is that they're taxed at lower rates. Qualified dividends are taxed at long-term capital gains tax rates, while ordinary dividends are taxed at ordinary income tax rates. As a refresher, ordinary income taxes work as follows.

The Internal Revenue Services (IRS) has created different tiers of income, along with their requisite rates, to help determine how much tax a filer has to pay at the end of the year. The tax brackets are marginal, which means if you earn $100,000 and are filing as a single person, your first $9,875 is taxed at 10%, the next $40,125 is taxed at 12%, and the rest of your income is taxed at 22%.

Ordinary income tax rates go as high as 37%, and this can add up if you earn money from your investments, especially stock market ones. Real estate investors usually get to deduct expenses, much like business owners do, but stock market investors don't. This is why the qualified dividend is a boon.

Capital gains refer to gains earned via the rise in asset prices. If you buy a stock for $4, and it rises to $10, you've earned a capital gain of $6. You capture capital gains when you sell a stock. This is a realized capital gain, as opposed to an unrealized one that remains on paper. Note that only realized capital gains are taxed.

If you've held the stock for less than a year before selling it, you'll pay short-term capital gains taxes. These capital gains will be taxed just like ordinary income tax. However, if you own the stock for more than a year, you're subject to long-term capital gains taxes. These taxes have just three tiers: Zero, 15%, and 20%.

Most retail investors will fall under the zero-tax rate because the limit is between $40,000 and $54,100 depending on how you file your taxes. Even if you pay the maximum rate of 20%, this is far lower than the equivalent income tax bracket, which will see you paying 30% or more.

Qualified dividends thus attract far lower rates than ordinary dividends. Your broker will provide you a form called the 1099-DIV at the end of the year, which will list the qualified and ordinary dividends you received. You'll need to use that information when you prepare your taxes.

Additional Taxes

There are two other taxes that are applicable to dividends. The first is a Medicare tax of 0.9% that you must pay if your income exceeds $200,000 if you're an ordinary filer, $250,000 if you're filing jointly, and $125,000 if married filing separately. Taxable dividend payments, whether qualified or ordinary, are subject to a net investment income tax of 3.8%. The thresholds for these are the same as those of the Medicare tax.

Retirement Accounts

Retirement accounts add a layer of complexity to the taxation process. Money held in a retirement account is taxed only when withdrawn. People usually withdraw it at the age of 59 ½, which is when the government stipulates one can withdraw money. Any withdrawals prior to that attract a 10% penalty.

Taxes on this money are charged at ordinary income levels. This means all dividend income you earn is automatically classified as ordinary, even if you satisfy the qualified dividends criteria. This has significant tax implications for most people. If you have a lengthy investment runway, then your dividends will likely compound enough so that the higher tax rates won't eat into your profits.

However, if you're going to have to withdraw your dividends within a few years, it makes more sense to hold dividend-paying investments in regular accounts. The reduced tax burden will make a difference at the end of the day. Given that everyone's tax situation is different, it's best to consult a tax advisor to figure out what works best for you.

Roth IRAs are taxed differently from Ordinary IRAs, and the method of withdrawal can play a huge role in your decision to hold dividend-paying instruments. If you're of age 59 ½ or older and have held the Roth for more than five years, you can withdraw your money tax-free, unlike in an Ordinary IRA, where you have to pay income taxes.

This means you'll pay no taxes on your dividend income, irrespective of its designation. Again, there are a few other rules to be aware of, so it's best to speak to a tax professional before deciding which way you'd like to go.

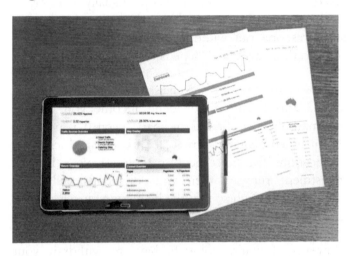

REIT Taxation

I haven't introduced REITs as of yet, so this material will seem premature. I'll talk about them in detail two chapters from now. You could read that chapter and return to this section. REITs are dividend-paying stocks that have a real estate focus. The important thing to know about REITs is that the dividend terminology changes a bit.

REITs pay ordinary dividends and return on capital or ROC dividends. ROC is a tricky concept for most people to figure out, so it's worth spending the time to understand it. Unlike a company that gets to decide the proportion of qualified versus ordinary dividends, REITs don't get to choose.

Instead, it's the IRS that designates ROC versus ordinary dividends. Ordinary dividends are taxed at income tax rates, while ROC payouts are considered tax-deferred, which means you won't pay taxes the moment you receive them and might potentially not have to pay any taxes at all.

This is because the IRS thinks of ROCs payouts as the REIT returning your money back to you. However, there is a catch. ROC payouts decrease your cost basis. For example, if you buy a REIT for $100 and receive an ROC dividend of $1, and you sell the REIT the next year for $105, then your capital gains should be (105-100) $5, right? Not quite.

The ROC decreases your cost basis by a dollar, meaning your capital gains are (105-99) $6. You'll pay capital gains taxes on this modified amount. Thus, you could buy a REIT for $100, sell it for $100 while receiving ROC payments, and still pay capital gains taxes. It sounds strange on paper, but it can happen over a long enough time period.

However, you can avoid paying taxes on ROC payouts for eternity. Here's how it works. As the ROC dividend keeps decreasing your cost basis, it isn't unrealistic to imagine a situation where your cost basis eventually reduces to zero. Every ROC payment from that point onward will attract long term capital gains taxes, which are capped at 20% as you've already learned.

You can avoid paying taxes on the ROC dividends you've captured before achieving zero-cost basis by never selling your REIT and passing it onto your heirs instead. When you do this, your heirs' cost basis in the investment is readjusted to the price the REIT was selling for on the day of your passing. As they continue to receive ROC dividends, their cost basis keeps decreasing, and they won't pay taxes until it hits zero. Thus, it's possible to pass REITs through generations like this and avoid ROC taxes. Of course, the trick is to choose a REIT that has that kind of staying power.

Something else to keep in mind is that the IRS has strict rules for defining the ROC component of an investment. The portion of a dividend payment that exceeds the REIT's net income is considered ROC. You might wonder how a REIT can pay a dividend greater than its net income? Well, that's why the world of REITs is a bit weird when it comes to taxation. You'll learn why this happens two chapters from now.

For now, understand that ROC taxation on REIT dividends makes them a different beast from routine dividend payments. Also note that, as with regular dividend payments, if you hold a REIT in an Ordinary IRA, they will be taxed as ordinary income, ROC or not. Roth IRAs will bring their own quirks into the mix and you can end up paying zero taxes on your REIT income, provided you withdraw your earnings at the right age.

This brings to a close out discussion of taxation. As you can see, it isn't a terribly complex topic, but there are a few nuances that you must be aware of. When in doubt, check with a tax professional for advice.

Chapter 8:
Bonus One - Living Off Your Dividends

The aim of investing in dividends and in the stock market in general is to ensure that you have enough money left for a comfortable retirement. Dividends can provide you with more than enough passive income to match your expenses. However, they take time to build, and a little bit of luck as well with regards to market positions.

For instance, you could do all the right things, but the market might crash just as you plan to retire. This means your portfolio yields might remain the same, but the amount of passive income you receive will be lower. Unfortunately, there's no way to guarantee you won't encounter a market crash, but it is possible to insulate yourself from its negative effects as much as possible.

Reducing Risk

In the earlier stages of your investing career, you should prioritize capital growth over dividend yields. While receiving cash every month sounds great, it isn't the best way to grow your portfolio. For instance, the stock market since 2009 has increased by an average of 15.41% per year. This doesn't include any dividends the stocks in the S&P 500 paid.

In contrast, even a high-yield dividend stock paying 10% seems much less. In the long run, capital gains are what creates wealth. Dividends are income, so you need to prioritize them according to your goals. When you're younger, you can work a job to earn income and don't necessarily need dividends, even if they're nice to have.

As you grow older, your ability to work diminishes, and you need income more than capital growth. Thus, you need to prioritize income, which means moving your money into investments that give you a good yield. Note that high yield by itself isn't worth it. Your money has to be safe. Thus, make sure you avoid any yield traps or stock with an artificially high yield, as I've discussed previously.

Sound investing principles still apply in retirement, but you'll just be screening for stocks or instruments that pay you high yields. There are many instruments that can pay you a safe four to five percent yield, so don't worry about not receiving enough money to pay your bills. Grow your capital as much as possible, then transfer it into high-yield stocks once you're ready to begin receiving passive income.

When to Transfer

The question of when you ought to transfer your holdings from capital growth-oriented dividend stocks to high-yield stocks is a tricky one. A lot depends on your personal situation. As a rule of thumb, you should begin moving your money at least two to five years prior to your planned retirement date.

The equation changes if you've held money in a retirement account. The tax disadvantages of holding dividends in those accounts means you're only going to pay additional money if you move your investments into high-yield instruments. Therefore, it's better to hold on until you're ready to withdraw the lump sum.

While moving a large sum of money into instruments all at once isn't advisable, it's the best option you have.

Needless to say, you should start monitoring the market around five years or so before retirement. Your goal with monitoring the market isn't to try to predict a crash, since that's impossible. Instead, your goal is to familiarize yourself with the possible instruments you could invest your money into. Start searching for them and begin understanding them.

Note that investing in individual companies in retirement is even more risky than investing in them pre-retirement, meaning you should emphasize sound investing principles even more. It might be a good idea to consider investing in funds and turning dividend income passive. However, if you have enough confidence in your abilities and have built a successful track record, there's no need to change.

I've already described the process by which you can calculate how much you'll need to have as principal to pay for your expenses. Obviously, everyone's financial situation differs, so you'll have to tailor those numbers for yourself. If you find that you cannot fully subsidize your retirement expenses via passive income, aim to pay for a percentage of expenses.

Also, you should focus on increasing your income from alternative sources, such as social security or a pension plan if your employer offers one. Note that delaying social security collections till the age of 67, as opposed to collecting at 62, can have massive capital implications for you. Delaying collection by five years will give you a higher standard of living.

Withdrawing Capital

Another approach you can take to ensure a healthy retirement is withdrawing four percent of your portfolio every year to pay for expenses. A withdrawal rate of four percent every year, coupled with dividend-assisted passive income, will result in you being able to rely on that money for close to 25 years.

You could also bucket your capital into different categories and rely on them to pay for certain expenses. For instance, one category of money could pay for living expenses. Since these are essential, you could dedicate the largest percentage of your portfolio to these investments. Given that you'll need this money at all times, you could also invest it in safe instruments.

Another bucket could pay for non-essential investments. You can take a few risks with this money and invest it in alternative higher-yield instruments that I'll highlight in the next chapter. If the market suffers a downturn, you won't be adversely affected since you can skip these expenses.

Preparation is the key to successfully living off your dividends. Make sure you estimate your expenses in retirement properly and include a good margin of safety within those numbers. Some people tend to get unrealistic with their estimates, which results in them falling short of their goals.

Chapter 9:
Bonus Two - Other Investments

Dividend stocks and funds are great, but there are other instruments you can invest in to earn dividend income. These instruments range from the safe to the speculative, so they aren't created equal. Make sure you understand the risks of investing in some of these instruments before choosing to go into them.

With that being said, let's take a look at one of the most popular investment instruments.

REITs

Real Estate Investment Trusts, or REITs, are a great way to invest in real estate without having to come up with the money to own it physically. Physical real estate requires you to invest a significant sum via a down payment and then draw a mortgage to finance the property's purchase. This means you need to overcome significant hurdles to own property. Once you own the property, there are additional needs to take care of, such as maintenance and so on.

If you're short of money, REITs offer you a great way to enter the real estate space. A REIT is a publicly traded company that receives preferential tax treatment from the IRS. They don't pay corporate taxes, which means the REIT's managing partners get to take home a greater share of company profits. The catch is that the IRS mandates REITs pay 90% of the profits back to investors as dividends.

The result is that REIT investors receive greater dividend yields from their investments. The average REIT pays out a yield of close to six percent compared to the average three percent that a stock does. Therefore, investors prioritizing income love REITs. The flip side is that REITs don't offer as much in capital gains as either physical real estate or stocks do.

This is because of the way a REIT is structured. Essentially, a REIT manages property and collects rents from it. It might even sell the property and capture a capital gain. but this doesn't happen all too often in a stable REIT. The aim is to generate property management fees (through rent payments, etc.) as much as possible.

Property in the United States is a lucrative investment, but local real estate factors govern the rate at which capital grows. Given the national exposure that large REITs have, capital gains tend to fluctuate, with one portion of the portfolio cancelling the other. This doesn't mean there are no capital gains, but it does mean that you can't expect your portfolio to grow at the same rate.

There are different kinds of REITs you can invest in. Let's take a look at which ones are the best.

REIT Types

A REIT can invest in all kinds of property. The types of investments range from residential, to commercial, and even raw land. For instance, there are REITS that specialize in investing in land reserved for marijuana growth. There are REITs that invest in land reserved for cell phone towers, agriculture, and so on. These REITs are broadly classified as equity REITs. They own a stake in the property they've invested in. and it's in their best interest to maintain and develop them.

The other kind of REIT you'll find is a mortgage REIT. These REITs act as financiers for building projects and earn money via the interest payments the developer pays. In short, they lend money to developers and earn interest.

Mortgage REITs are complex companies and might not be suited to most people. They engage in financial engineering, and analyzing them isn't the easiest thing to do. For the most part, they invest in mortgage-backed securities and other asset-backed instruments that are opaque, without liquid markets. This is why equity REITs are far easier to make sense of.

Within the equity REIT space, there are multiple types of properties you'll find REITs investing in. For example, you could have companies investing in residential and commercial properties. Some REITs invest in just commercial shopping facilities. such as malls and shopping centers, while others invest solely in office space, and so on.

Every REIT has its own strategy, and you should take the time to understand them thoroughly.

Accounting Quirks

One of the things that most beginner investors struggle to understand is REIT accounting, especially depreciation. REITs have to follow the general accounting principles laid out for all companies in the United States, but these principles often leave REITs in a strange position.

Look through a selection of REITs and you'll find that many of them have payout ratios greater than 100%. This makes no sense at all, given that REITs will pay this amount for many years consistently. So, where's the money coming from?

This anomaly occurs due to the way asset depreciation is handled. When we looked at this in the previous example, depreciating a piece of furniture made sense. However, a REITs major asset is real estate. This asset appreciates over time, and doesn't depreciate unless the REIT mismanages it.

Thus, the depreciation expense the REIT logs is completely false. However, their income statements include this deduction anyway because accounting principles mandate it. As such, the bottom-line net income is well off the true cash earnings that the REIT posts. Investors should always look at the cash flow statement when looking at REIT earnings, since the income statement doesn't provide much guidance.

This is also why the IRS handled ROC the way it does. Any income over the stated net income is ROC. REITs that have a ton of old properties on their books will have written down their properties to almost zero, but will be earning large cash flow on them. The large depreciation expense will ensure that ROC dividends are high and investors benefit from this.

Take care when analyzing metrics such as return on assets (ROA) on a REIT. ROA is calculated by dividing the net income by total assets, but both numbers are useless when looking at a REIT thanks to the way they're accounted for. Assets are written down instead of being inflated, and net income includes depreciation, which is non-existent.

Incidentally, depreciation is an advantage when you own physical real estate, since it allows you to lower your net income earned from the property on paper. Many property owners take advantage of this, along with other tax write-offs, to lower their taxes. These advantages aren't available to REIT investors since they don't own property. Instead, they own shares in a company that owns property.

Thus, if you have enough money to own physical property and would like the security it provides, along with the rental income, consider buying it instead of investing that money in a REIT. The tax write-offs you'll receive will make it worth your while more than a REIT. However, if passive income is your primary goal, then nothing beats a REIT.

Something else to consider when owning a REIT is that they don't pay 90% of their rental income to investors. They pay 90% of their profits, meaning that they subtract their costs from the rental income and return 90% of that number to investors. Compare the dividend payout to revenues received by the REIT. A large discrepancy between the numbers indicates a management that is keener on padding their pockets instead of running a good business.

You can invest in a REIT index via an index fund as well. The yields will be lower, but you'll turn your investment completely passive. Overall, REITs are an excellent investment for those looking to earn passive income.

Covered Call Funds

Covered calls are an options trading strategy that is designed to produce steady income in a portfolio. The idea is to own a stock and then earn a synthetic dividend from it, even if it doesn't pay a dividend.

Here's how it works. Let's say you buy 50 shares of Amazon. Amazon doesn't pay a dividend, but you'd like to earn cash flow from your stock purchase. The way you do this is by writing or selling a call option. Call option buyers have the right to buy the stock at a certain price, and they make money when the stock price rises. Conversely, call writers make money as long as the price of the stock remains below the trigger price attached to the call.

When an investor writes a call, they receive a premium, which is the cost that the buyer pays to the seller. All options expire at a certain point. If the stock remains below the trigger price before the expiry date, the writer keeps the premium and the buyer is out of luck, receiving nothing.

However, if the stock rises above the call trigger price before expiry, the seller has to sell the stock they own to the buyer at the trigger price. Thus, the writer loses their position in the stock. I appreciate that this might be complicated if you've never heard of options or derivatives, but that's my point. Covered calls need specialized management, and most investors run towards them without understanding what's actually happening behind the scenes.

You'll hear a lot about covered calls, specifically QYLD, that yields 13% or more. This yield is true, and it isn't engineered via price drops. However, QYLD provides almost zero capital gains. What's more, it suffers from routine capital losses, which renders the 13% yield moot. There's no point earning 13% on a shrinking sum of capital.

Devoting a small portion of your portfolio to these funds is wise, but don't sweat it if you aren't invested in them. The high yields are balanced out by highly likely capital losses.

Other Instruments

Talk of dividends and you'll eventually run into BDCs, MLPs, and closed-end funds. BDCs are business development companies, and they make money by investing in financially distressed companies. They try to turn these operations around and fuel them with debt, then collect dividends from these turnaround companies and pass them onto their investors.

BDCs business models resemble what corporate raiders back in the day used to do. Those people would saddle their target companies with debt, extract whatever they could, and either sell the company for parts or sell it for a profit. Aside from the ethical implications of this model, most turnarounds don't work, and these BDCs can be illiquid. However, exceptions do exist, and you can find good ones that pay huge dividends.

Non-traded BDCs have heavy fees, low liquidity, and very little transparency. Those three strikes make it hard to justify keeping them in your investment lineup.

MLPs are typically found in the natural resources sector. An oil company has varied operations and needs some place to store its delivery assets, such as pipelines and other machinery. An MLP is a company that is contracted to the parent on paper, while the parent holds all the cards.

Some MLPs are wonderful investments. However, the majority of them are risky and subject to dissolution by their parents at any point in time. If you're confident of being able to figure out their business models, then they are viable investments, but there are easier ways to make money.

Contracts for difference or CFDs allow you to invest in instruments that mimic the movements of stocks. For instance, let's say you wished to invest in an index fund that tracks the movement of the Hong Kong stock market. Instead of buying an index fund with a broker from that part of the world, you can simply buy a CFD which gives you all the advantages of the original instrument. The CFD will move in accordance with the stock index and pay you whatever dividends the index fund pays its investors. Note that CFDs are currently not legal in the United States.

Lastly, we have closed-end funds, which are excellent investments. Their biggest draw is that, unlike mutual funds that always accept new investors, these funds are closed. This results in their prices trading at a discount to their net asset value (NAV). Investors buy in thinking they're receiving a dollar for a nickel as a result.

The discount always persists because they aren't open to new investors. Like MLPs, some closed-end funds are great investments, but most of them are savvy marketing machines. Once again, at the end of the day, there's easier ways of making money.

Conclusion

Dividend investing is one of the most lucrative ways of growing your money in the markets. However, it takes time, and it certainly isn't a get-rich-quick scheme. You need to begin by figuring out how much you'd like to earn once you retire and use the calculator provided in this book to arrive at your ideal portfolio value.

From there, play around with how much you can invest every month and you'll develop a clear plan to financial success. Many investors in the stock market lack patience and end up sabotaging themselves. Thanks to the fear of missing out and general fear of the markets, investors end up selling at the worst possible times and do a lot of damage to themselves.

Take care to review the material in this book regularly, since it goes far beyond investment strategies. At various points, I've noted the mindset you need to possess to succeed in the markets. Without the right mindset, you're unlikely to hold onto your investment for long enough to make a difference.

You can be an active or a passive investor since both approaches have their merits. While active investment sounds like something everyone would be interested in, it isn't easy to pull off. You need lots of time and dedication to make that strategy work. For most investors, passive investing makes a lot more sense, since you'll manage to earn dividends and grow your money passively.

When the time comes, start moving your money into higher-yielding instruments with a view to earn higher payouts every month. If you can't cover all of your living expenses, try to cover a portion of them and work on increasing other sources of income. Remember to DRIP your dividends into your investments, and that you'll be liable for taxes even if you DRIP your payouts back into your stock positions.

As we arrive at the end of this book, I hope you're as excited as I am about the journey you're going to embark on! If you feel this book taught you something you previously weren't aware of, please let me know by leaving me a review and letting me know what you think.

I wish you all the profits and steady dividends in the

world! Happy investing!

References

Desjardins, J. (2018, February 6). The Power of Dividend Investing. Visual Capitalist. https://www.visualcapitalist.com/power-dividend-investing/

Edwards, J. (2021, June 2). The Benefits of High-Dividend Yielding Stocks. Investopedia. https://www.investopedia.com/articles/investing/090715/best-places-find-highdividend-yield-stocks.asp

Kennon, J. (2021, June 2). What Is Dividend Investing? The Balance. https://www.thebalance.com/what-is-dividend-investing-357437

Muller, C. (2021, June 2). How To Invest In Dividend Stocks The Right Way. Money under 30. https://www.moneyunder30.com/how-to-invest-in-dividend-stocks

Sullivan, B. (2020, October 19). Guide To Dividend Investing For Beginners. Forbes Advisor. https://www.forbes.com/advisor/investing/dividend-investing/

Tahiri, A. (2019). The 3 Biggest Misconceptions of Dividend Stocks. Investopedia. https://www.investopedia.com/articles/investing/082015/3-biggest-misconceptions-dividend-stocks.asp

All images from Pixabay

Other Promoted Authors

M.L. PILGRIM

S. K. PILGRIM

I.K. BUTCHER

ABOUT THE AUTHOR

M. L. Pilgrim lost millions when he was starting as an entrepreneur but only his consistent belief in the power of the subconscious mind has brought him to his success. He is very active investing with majority of his portfolio in precious metals and stocks. Also, he invests in bonds, mutual funds, UITFs, and in other businesses in real estate, power generation, banking, logistics, retail, and telecommunications.

He worked across 10 countries always fascinated with the beauty of nature, culture, and traditions. He is a versatile author writing both fiction and non-fiction. He is a traveler, a dedicated father, a loving son, and a responsible brother.

He strongly believes that everyone can succeed both in business, relationships, society, and other aspects if they only have the right information and knowledge on how to use that information properly.

M. L. Pilgrim uses a pen name as he doesn't want to show himself as a definitive expert. Instead, he is in this journey with his readers like a "pilgrim" and wants to travel with them and share their experiences.

Reach M. L. Pilgrim in mlpilgrim.author@gmail.com. Cheers!

Or subscribe to his newsletter for latest updates on his investment books.

BOOKS BY THIS AUTHOR

THE PEOPLE'S GOLD: EVERYONE, EVERYWHERE, EVERY TIME! A Beginner's Practical Guide on All You Need to Know on How to Profit from Gold

Don't have gold in your investment portfolio? Here's why you're missing out.

Is gold just for the rich?

Is it irrelevant in this highly digital economy?

Will it be of any use to your already diversified portfolio?

With prices at thousands of dollars for a few grams, gold is an expensive element.

You'd have good reason to believe that it's only something the wealthy would buy, and probably just as a part of their collection of expensive things.

But gold is much more than a material for luxurious jewelry or for ornate decorations.
Nowadays, gold is considered a safe haven for investors in an increasingly volatile market.

Some investors invest in gold when they foresee a recession, inflation, or uncertainty. Others hold on to gold to preserve wealth, while having a vehicle to pass it on to future generations.

In short, because uncertainty is inherent in any investment and in any economy, gold can serve as insurance in case of economic or political disasters.

Even in a highly digitized economy, gold continues to be attractive because it's a tangible asset that can still be of value, even if our entire monetary system collapses.

Fortunately, gone are the days when you had to pan for gold in a river, under the heat of the sun, with the possibility of ending up with nothing but a severe sunburn.

In today's economy, gold is easier to access and more affordable as well.

There are several ways to invest in gold that require nothing more than a computer, an internet connection, and a reasonable amount of money.

Don't lose out on the benefits of gold in your portfolio, even if you don't have billions of dollars to spare.

In THE PEOPLE'S GOLD: EVERYONE, EVERYWHERE, EVERY TIME!, YOU WILL DISCOVER:

- A **step-by-step guide** to getting started with gold investments, which you can follow even without any investing background
- How to legitimately invest in gold with **less than $100**
- **How much of your portfolio to invest in gold** so you don't lose out on market gains, but you still protect yourself enough in case of a severe downturn

- An **easy and accessible way to invest** in gold without having to worry about storage and theft
- How to tell real versus fake gold, and other smart ways to **protect yourself from gold scammers**
- Have a better understanding of your profile as a gold investor
- The varying reasons for investing in gold, and how they affect your investment strategy
- Know the different types of gold investors and see which one you can identify yourself the most
- **Bonus chapter**: Practical tips for investing in silver that could augment your portfolio even more

AND MUCH MORE.

Whether you think the economy as we know it will collapse in the foreseeable future, or you're just looking for a hedge against low interest rates, gold offers you this protection and more.

Even if you think your portfolio is already diversified enough, with stocks, bonds, real estate, and more, gold can still make a valuable addition to your portfolio.

Its unique qualities & ability to hedge against both equities & fixed income securities offer an extra layer of diversification & protection, especially for the most extreme cases.

Don't wait until the economic system collapses. Get some gold now and ensure that you're financially protected in case anything ever happens.

If you want to protect your finances & prepare for an uncertain future with a tangible, safe, & reliable asset, then grab a copy right now!

SCAN ME

EL ORO DE LA GENTE: ¡para todos, en todas partes, en todo momento! Sección extra: cómo vender plata

D¿No tienes oro en tu cartera de inversiones? Te proporcionamos la explicación de por qué te lo estás perdiendo.

¿Es el oro solo para los ricos?

¿Es irrelevante en esta economía tan digital?

¿Será útil para tu cartera de inversiones ya diversificada?

Con precios de miles de dólares por unos pocos gramos, el oro es un elemento caro.

Tendrías buenas razones para creer que es algo que solo comprarían los ricos, y probablemente solo como parte de su colección de cosas caras.

Pero el oro es mucho más que un material para joyas lujosas o para decoraciones ornamentales.

Hoy en día, el oro se considera un refugio seguro para los inversores en un mercado cada vez más volátil.

Algunos inversores invierten en oro cuando prevén una recesión, inflación o incertidumbre. Otros se aferran al oro para preservar su riqueza y tener un vehículo para transmitirla a las generaciones futuras.

I En resumen, dado que la incertidumbre es inherente a cualquier inversión y a cualquier economía, el oro puede servir de seguro en caso de desastres económicos o políticos.

Incluso en una economía altamente digitalizada, el oro sigue siendo atractivo porque es un activo tangible que puede seguir teniendo valor, incluso si todo nuestro sistema monetario se derrumba.

Afortunadamente, ya han pasado los días en los que había que buscar oro en un río, bajo el calor del sol, con la posibilidad de acabar solo con una grave quemadura solar.

En la economía actual, el oro es más fácil de conseguir y también más asequible.

Hay varias formas de invertir en oro que no requieren más que un ordenador, una conexión a Internet y una cantidad razonable de dinero.

No te pierdas las ventajas del oro en tu cartera de inversiones, aunque no tengas miles de millones de dólares de sobra.

En *Oro para la clase media*, descubrirás:

- Una**guía de pasos a seguir** sobre cómo comenzar a invertir en oro, que puedes seguir incluso sin ningún tipo de experiencia en inversiones.
- Cómo invertir legítimamente en oro >con menos de 100 dólares
- Por qué **necesitas comprar oro físico** si estás invirtiendo en oro por esta razón

- **Cuánto de tu cartera de inversiones debes gastar en oro** para no perder las ganancias del mercado, pero aún así protegerte lo suficiente en caso de una recesión severa.

- Una **forma fácil y accesible de invertir** en oro sin que tengas que preocuparte por su almacenamiento y posible robo.

- Cómo distinguir el oro auténtico del falso, y otras estrategias inteligentes **que te permitirán protegerte de los estafadores de oro.**

- Las diferentes razones para invertir en oro y la manera en que estas afectan tu estrategia de inversión

- **Capítulo extra:**consejos prácticos para invertir en plata que podrían aumentar aún más tu cartera de inversiones.

Y mucho mas.

Ya sea que pienses que la economía tal como la conocemos colapsará en el futuro próximo, o simplemente estás buscando una cobertura contra las bajas tasas de interés, el oro te ofrece esta protección y más.

Incluso si crees que tu cartera de inversiones ya está lo suficientemente diversificada, con acciones, bonos, bienes raíces y demás, el oro aún puede ser una valiosa adición a tu cartera.

Sus cualidades únicas y su capacidad para protegerte tanto de la renta variable como de la renta fija ofrecen una capa adicional de diversificación y protección, especialmente para los casos más extremos.

No esperes a que el sistema económico colapse. Obtén algo de oro ahora y asegúrate de estar protegido financieramente en caso de que algo suceda.

Si quieres proteger tus finanzas y prepararte para un futuro incierto con un activo tangible, seguro y fiable, desplázate hacia arriba y haz clic en el botón "Añadir a la cesta" ahora mismo.

What do you know about investing in Silver?

The decision to start a project or take the first steps in the path of investment may be difficult but choosing the right investment and the field that matches your ambitions and needs is much more difficult. Perhaps this fear comes from the idea that you are here at risk of loss. You can easily lose everything that you have gathered in your life, but there is always light in the midst of all this.

Silver is not very much traded in the world, but because people love imitation. "See, this person has succeeded in trading gold, let's be gold traders like him." This is the main reason for loss. Success stories and money of others tempt you, so you start running towards it without awareness even though there are hundreds of fields to choose from.

In this book, we will show you the most important points, methods, strategies, and tips that will give you the best start as a silver trader. Outlined among the chapters of this book, you will learn about silver investing across the following topics:

✓ **Advantages** of Trading in Silver

✓ **Disadvantages** of Trading in Silver

✓ Is trading in Silver **Profitable**?

✓ How to Start the Business?

✓ Where to Trade Silver?

✓ **Silver Trading Strategies**

We did not write these tips in a night or two and did not discover them by chance, we have already encountered them and have proven their effectiveness, and we have already seen many amazing stories thanks to them and we would like to give you the opportunity to be among them, to use your chances in life!

So, grab a copy now of this book and check out our exciting bonuses and free books that you can avail!

SCAN ME

Are you ready for an inside look at the explosive new trend in precious metals?

Have you had enough of stocks and bonds? Are you tired of watching your rate of return crawl slower than inflation? Have you always wished that you could watch your investments multiply?

Platinum and palladium have earning potentials beyond anything else on the market now, and they're easier to invest in than ever before.

If you don't know much about these rare metals, you are not alone. Palladium and platinum have historically been overlooked, shunned in favor of the better known metals, gold and silver. But now, these natural resources are coming into their rightful due. With demand for them exploding, they are truly 'precious' metals.

So, what makes these materials so special? They are not just for jewelry and watches. Both platinum and palladium can be used as a catalyst in electric vehicles and fuel cell vehicles, to improve lithium oxygen and lithium sulphur car batteries, and are used to produce green hydrogen through electrolysis.

With an increasing global shift toward renewable energy and eco-friendly vehicles, the demand for these two metals is skyrocketing and the only way to go is up from here. Platinum is considerably more rare than gold, and more expensive to mine. However, despite being costly to supply, investment in platinum is heavily discounted at the moment. Palladium's value has also increased greatly, making these two metals ones you want to be involved with!

Inside Best Ways to Invest in Platinum and Palladium, you will discover:

- Why these rare and precious metals should be in every investor's portfolio

- New and innovative ways that scientists are using both palladium and platinum

- How platinum and palladium metal compare to gold and silver as a vehicle for your hard-earned money

- Expert trading strategies to make sure you earn the highest possible profit while investing in precious metals

- The pros and cons of purchasing palladium bullion directly from a mint

- How and why to invest in a palladium ETF and platinum ETF

- Where and when to find the best platinum bars price

- Step-by-step guides through websites and apps showing you how to invest in precious metals

- What to expect in the future for your palladium and platinum buy

- How to begin with only $20 to invest for platinum investing

- Bonus insider tips on rhodium, another hot new trend in precious metals

And much more!

The palladium element and platinum bars have long been ignored by investors focused on the higher-volume gold and silver markets—but soon they won't be so easy to overlook. Get in on these metals now, before their prices skyrocket. You'll thank yourself in ten years when you're looking at your bank account and seeing all the zeros before the dot.

Don't miss out on the most exciting financial opportunity that's available today. Scroll up and one-click *Best Ways to Invest in Platinum and Palladium* to start on your investment journey now!

BEST WAYS TO INVEST IN GOLD FOR BEGINNERS: QUICK GUIDE FOR LEARNING AND INVESTING IN GOLD. (BONUS: 14 WAYS TO ESTABLISH REAL GOLD FROM FAKE GOLD AND MORE!)

Gold has kept a great value for thousands of years, and until this day it still occupies this high position, due to its properties that make it at the forefront of precious metals.

As it still retains its value throughout the ages, and the belief that is embedded in people's minds is that gold is the only way to pass and conserve wealth from one generation to another.

In times of political and economic tension as well as natural disasters, investors resort to buying gold as a safe haven in the markets and as a store of value, and it is also used as a hedge against high inflation. If you want gold to be part of your investment portfolio, you can choose from several investment options in gold, each of which has different investment characteristics. In this book, we offer many ways to invest in gold, tips to make the greatest possible start and the guide by which you can avoid fraud. We hope that we could help you, best of luck!

Don't Forget to <u>Claim</u> your FREE ebook!

BEST WAYS TO INVEST MONEY DURING COVID-19:
MAKE MONEY AT HOME

There are many things we can do during the pandemic and the most productive of all is to invest it wisely. Check out this book for some tips and guidance.

SCAN ME

<u>HOW TO UNDERSTAND THE SUBCONSCIOUS MIND:
UNLOCK, UNLEASH, AND LET IT TRANSFORM YOU!</u>

What do you know about the subconscious mind?

Do you want to know more about its characteristics? It is within us, but it is elusive in many aspects. So, careful understanding of the subconscious mind will bring us many benefits.

This book will share about the ff:

- What is the subconscious mind?
- Its relationship with the conscious mind
- Methods of connecting with the subconscious mind
- Secrets of the subconscious mind
- The rules of the subconscious mind
- Using your subconscious mind to achieve your goals
- Programming the subconscious mind
- How to achieve sleep miracles
- Controlling your subconscious mind

So, what are you waiting for? Check out this informative yet insightful book in unleashing this mysterious power within ourselves.

HOW TO THRIVE IN AWKWARD CONVERSATIONS:
LEARN THE ART OF SPEAKING WITH SKILL AND
CONSIDERATION (BONUS! 10 TIPS TO IMPROVE
YOUR CONVERSATION SKILLS!)

Have you ever found yourself in the middle of an Awkward Conversation?

Conversation is an art of dealing and communicating with others. Effective Communication aims to build understanding and acceptance - not conflict. However, there is that other type of conversation - *the awkward conversation.*

When you are in the midst of an embarrassing moment, you see yourself in a situation you wished you were not. Hence, knowing what to do exactly in those moments will prepare you for the worst.

This book will help you on the ff:
- Importance of Speaking Tactfully
- What makes conversations awkward and how to avoid them?

- How to have perfect conversation with your partner?
- How to handle a conversation with your parents?
- Business and work conversations
- General Tips and Tricks to be a top speaker

Grab a copy of this book and start your journey into more assertive, confident, and tactful!

HOW TO SAY NO TO YOURSELF: CONQUERING INTERMITTENT FASTING 101- THE COMPLETE GUIDE FOR BEGINNERS & BUSY PEOPLE (BONUS: NO-STRESS 30-DAY SIMPLE PLAN, MEAL PREPARATIONS, COOKBOOK AND MORE!)

Intermittent fasting is currently one of the most popular health and fitness trends in the world. It will teach you the unique process of following alternative fasting and feeding cycles.

This book contains proven steps and strategies on how to intermittently fast for weight loss and also examines the concept of clean nutrition.

By reading it, you will learn practical and proven arts and practices that, if followed religiously, will create a young, vibrant, exuberant, radiant and totally different being.

Do you have to lose weight? Are you trying to adapt to that new outfit for the summer? But you don't want to fall in love with those diets and lose weight with the quick tricks of the past, you need something that really stands the test of time. Much more than a diet, you need a change in lifestyle. This is exactly what the 30-day intermittent fasting challenge offers. Intermittent fasting can restart and restore the body, helping to put metabolic processes back on track. Fasting teaches your body to burn fat instead of complex carbohydrates.

With your body poised and ready to burn fat for fuel, stubborn fatty deposits like your belly, arms and legs will evaporate quickly! It may sound too good to be true, but only by regulating the body through a dedicated and consistent fasting regimen - this is truly possible! This book provides you with the knowledge, background, and recipes to successfully perform your intermittent fasting regime over the course of 30 days.

In this book you will get:

Why fast?

What is intermittent fasting?

Intermittent fasting and your hormones

Intermittent fasting and weight loss

Eat Healthily

The Keto diet

Autophagy and intermittent fasting

Pagan's diet

Intermittent fasting methods

Intermediate fasting benefits

Dangers of intermittent fasting

Intermittent fasting programs

And, in essence, everything you need to learn how to apply the practice of intermittent fasting to your life program to reap immense intrinsic benefits and thus become a healthier, happier, better and, yes, richer being.

SCAN ME

THE BOY WHO SPEAKS 100 LANGUAGES AND HELPS MANY PEOPLE ALL OVER THE WORLD

It is his 7th birthday; he got a gift. Little did he know what this gift can do for him … Where will he go? What can he do? Can Sephas save the day?

KENOSIS BOOKS: BE THE BEST YOU – SELF-IMPROVEMENT SERIES

SUBSCRIBE AND GET YOUR FREE eBOOK!

If you want to improve the quality of your attention and are willing to do other means to improve your focus and concentration, then this book will definitely help you in that. This book contains the ff:

1. Top Foods to increase your Focus and Concentration

2. Foods you can intake daily to improve your focus

3. Best Juices to Improve your focus

4. Healthy Habits and Eating Style to Improve Focus

..... and much more!

So take action, and scan the QR CODE *and/or* Subscribe *to our* **Kenosis Books - Be The Best You: Self-Improvement Series** *mailing list and be updated in our latest books and promotions!*

ABOUT THE AUTHOR

S.K. Pilgrim loves nature, travelling, food, and learning. He is a sport buff and loves running a lot. As a marathoner, he believes that keeping himself in good shape not only improves his running but also other aspects of his life. He loves reading books as well as writing them.

S.K. Pilgrim has a full-time job as senior leader in a multinational company. He is very passionate in coaching, training, and organizational development. He never gives up on any talent until they progress and improve to their potential!

Reach SK Pilgrim and our other authors in
kenosisbooks@gmail.com

Cheers!

BOOK BY THIS AUTHOR

GIGA-ENERGY: HIGH ENERGY FOOD - TURN-AWAY
FROM SWEETS AND ENERGY DRINKS BONUS: LOW
CHOLESTEROL AND LOW SUGAR ENERGY
BOOSTERS

LOW ON ENERGY? HOW LONG CAN YOU SUSTAIN YOUR ENERGY?

Daily tasks and labor require a lot of energy but ending up on the vicious cycle of coffee, sweets, and high-energy drinks is detrimental to our health.

This book aims to share with you alternative sources of energy that will make you more energetic and last longer through more sustainable and healthy means.

- Instant Energy Boosters
- Long-term Energy Boosters
- Plant-Based Energy Boosters

- Juices and Smoothies Energy Boosters
- Daily Routines to Maintain Energy Levels
- Faster Metabolism and Weight Loss
- Energy-packed Breakfast
- and Much Much More!
- BONUS
  - Low-cholesterol Energy Boosters
  - Low-sugar Energy Boosters

Grab a copy of this book and let it lead you to **GIGA-ENERGY** lifestyle!

ABOUT THE AUTHOR

I.K. Butcher's passion for building a conducive workplace started when he was in university. He began studying people development and practiced it firsthand. He led teams not only into developing themselves but also directing them into purpose – most especially, the socially oriented one.

Butcher continued this passion when he moved to a consumer goods company after he achieved his university degree. For 12 years, he learned sales, capability building, and business development. He travelled to various places both domestically and internationally to hone his skills and share his lessons to new employees who have begun in their careers.

Butcher believes that one needs to learn multitudes of skills to really excel in an organization and that he is very much willing to share his experiences to help those who are really serious about such an endeavor.

Reach I. K. Butcher and our other authors in
kenosisbooks@gmail.com!

BOOK BY THIS AUTHOR

MANAGING UPWARDS: THE BEGINNER'S GUIDE IN
MANAGING YOUR BOSS (BONUS: THE SOFT SIDE:
HOW TO WIN YOUR BOSS BY BUILDING A
FRIENDLY RELATIONSHIP)

*Have you been struggling with your boss? Are you a start out
with the management skills to workplace excellence? Do you
simply fancy the topic and wish to be armed with the artillery
for Managing your Boss?*

Whatever the category you find yourself in, this book is poised to
arm you with all the necessary strategies for starting and
maintaining a healthy and synergistic relationship with your boss in
such a way that your personal goals, that of your boss, and the
overall objectives of your company are met.

Outlined in well thought of moves, you will be led through four
exciting journeys of

✓   Self-identification, skill discovery and skill optimization

✓   Identifying the personal traits, strengths, weaknesses, and context of your boss

✓   Knowing the company, what it stands for, your role and that of your boss

✓   Bridging the gap where stark differences exist

The major chapters all end with action points, step to take to ensure proper use of the information you're provided with. For the young, for the experienced, for whoever seeks to stand out and succeed in the workplace, this is the book for you.

So, grab a copy now of this book and check out our exciting bonuses and free books that you can avail!

SUBSCRIBE AND GET YOUR FREE eBOOK!

Don't Forget to <u>Claim</u> your FREE eBook!

Made in United States
Troutdale, OR
12/20/2024